AN DODGE AND BURN 2021–23 VIDEO TRANSCRIPT: I CAN'T REMEMBER WHEN EXACTLY, BUT IT WAS MANY MA

DODGE AND/OR BURN

Lisa Tan

RS AGO THAT I HAPPENED TO BE ON A FLIGHT TO LOS ANGELES ON THE 4TH OF JULY. THE PLANE APPROAC

CITY JUST AS NIGHT FELL GIVING ME A CHANCE TO SEE FIREWORKS FROM MY WINDOW SEAT. IT WAS EQUAL

TIFUL AND DISTURBING. IT LOOKED LIKE A WAR ZONE. LOS ANGELES INTERNATIONAL AIRPORT IS ONLY TW

LISA TAN AT ACCELERATOR

4

Therese Kellner
curator at Accelerator

ETERS AWAY FROM THE COAST. ANY FIGHT DESTINED FOR LAX HEADS IN THE DIRECTION OF THE PACIFIC O

I was first introduced to Oliver Sacks's diagram showing different manifestations of migraine by Lisa Tan. We had decided to collaborate on a solo presentation of her work across Accelerator's two galleries. While visiting her studio, she showed me a book by the British neurologist, which was opened to a page with an illustration entitled *Physiological Organisation of Migraines*. "What do you see?" The way the question was posed indicated she expected a particular answer. A map? "Isn't it interesting that he chose to describe migraine with a diagram that looks like a floor plan?" I began to discern elements that looked familiar. Tan continued: "If I overlay it on top of a floor plan of Accelerator's two galleries, it fits remarkably well. I have this hunch to use Sacks's diagram as the driver for the entire exhibition." This became the starting point for *Dodge and/or Burn* at Accelerator. Sacks's diagram was used as a template for the installation *Promise or Threat* (2023) and served as the exhibition's organizing principle. The walls, made of standard wood studs, created a series of open rooms; within this structure, the artist presented the video installation *Dodge and Burn* (2021–2023), photographs from the *Waiting Room* series (2019–2023), sculptural light boxes comprising the work *Pa* (2023), and the text-based self-portraits of *Letters from Dr Bamberger* (2001–2012).

For the exhibition, Tan looked at the intersection between the nervous system and interior life as a way of examining how art operates, uncertainty, and the formation of the self. The purpose of this publication is not to detail the exhibition and the works in it, but to offer something that exists in the thought-universe it initiates. The book comprises images from *Dodge and/or Burn* alongside essays by three authors whose work has, as Tan puts it, "changed the way I think on a psychobiological level." Writer Haytham el-Wardany, psychoanalyst Charlotta Björklind, and artist Asier Mendizabal are all active in some of the exhibition's associative fields: literature, psychology, and visual art. Using their respective practices as a point of departure, the authors respond to the exhibition accordingly.

In a gesture that animated her long-standing preoccupation with the relationship between subjectivity and representation,[1] Tan turned Sacks's hand-drawn diagram into an unscripted journey. Visitors to Accelerator navigated through the different zones of the exhibition, making their own path through the system of open walls, which divided works across both rooms—some pieces abided by the existing architecture, while others were hung in accordance with the superimposed partitions of Sacks's diagram. From this arrangement, an analogy arose to human cognitive processes and the way we represent them in terms of space, overlap, and orientation. Our perception involves the interaction of billions of neurons from different parts of the brain, which is itself plastic, constantly creating new neural connections.

1 In this relationship lies the question: How can we ever articulate, capture, and convey a true image of ourselves or anyone else? Migraine is a highly subjective experience that varies from person to person. If you suffer from a neurological disorder or illness, you need to be able to find the right language to explain your condition and receive adequate treatment. We are at the mercy of language or (to borrow a term from author Ursula K. Le Guin) the carrier bag of words we carry around with us in order to create narratives of ourselves and the world around us.

We *are* and simultaneously *come into being* through what we occupy ourselves with.[2] Similarly, each of the works interacted with one another from different

2 In 2004, Oliver Sacks viewed with optimism the then relatively new neuroscience tendencies: "Instead of seeing the brain as rigid, fixed in mode, . . . there is now a much more biological and powerful notion of 'experiential selection,' of experience literally shaping the connectivity and function of the brain." Oliver Sacks, "In the River of Consciousness," *New York Review of Books*, January 15, 2004.

spatial positions in a totality that *came into being* through every viewer's choice of movement and attention while absorbing the exhibition. This gesture mirrors the overlapping of inner and outer life, the misalignment of subjective experience and any attempt to represent it, and the negotiation between the mind and the brain. These are aspects that Björklind and Mendizabal develop in their contributions to the publication. Describing how we live in an interface, Björklind explores the relationship between the body's materiality and our inner psychic reality. Mendizabal writes of the overlapping of the brain and the mind as a paradoxical double space, which were united by the artist's voice that resonated in the galleries at Accelerator—a voice he describes as simultaneously taking place in the visitor's mental space. The monologue printed at the top of this book is a transcript of that voice, which is the artist's own, heard in the voice-over to her video *Dodge and Burn*. The work's title refers to a darkroom technique for manipulating a photograph by darkening or lightening select areas,[3] but Tan also makes use of the words' other mean-

3 In other words, this reference serves as a reminder that all images are constructs. Writer and critic Susan Sontag repeatedly asserted that every photographic representation is a subjective framing of reality that inevitably excludes other narratives.

ings, related to quick movement, burning heat, and exhaustion. The video is dominated by an impassive voice that propels the narrative forward and, in the installation, spilled out across the exhibition spaces. A second monitor, located in a zone where the dull whirring sound of an airplane cabin could also be heard (or felt), displayed the video installation's other channel. Excerpts from *Dodge and Burn*'s voice-over flashed or crawled across the screen in dislocated sequences made up of fragments attuned to body, time, emotion, and place—the core parameters of consciousness that determine how we navigate the world.[4]

4 Tan has employed gestures of dislocation and distortions of scale to create an element of displacement in the exhibition. Through spatially unfolding familiar forms and symbols such as letters, signage, and famous historical artworks, Tan makes the familiar unplaceable, causing us, for instance, to ransack our memory banks or activate language centers in the brain in order to put together the dispersed letters of *Pa*.

Sacks's work has inarguably impacted the field of neurology and entered into popular notions around the inner workings of the brain. In his early years as a practicing neurologist, the technology we have today to look inside the brain was unavailable. Instead, Sacks observed the brain by actively and sensitively listening to his patients. A parallel emerges here with el-Wardany's contribution, which closes this publication. In the second part of his story, the narrator describes an experience of listening to an interview and becoming alert to the audible breath of the interviewee heard between his verbalized answers.

ON THE RUNWAY. PLANES FROM THE NORTH, TURN EAST, AND THEN CURVE WEST OVER DOWNTOWN LOS ANGELE

When *intellect can't keep up with what touches us*,[5] perhaps it is the nonverbal voice,

5 A phrase from Tan's video *Dodge and Burn.*

which sometimes slips out with the breath between words, and at other times can just be felt as a hunch, that can guide us through a myriad of uncertain situations and encounters.

Physiological Organisation of Migraines 203

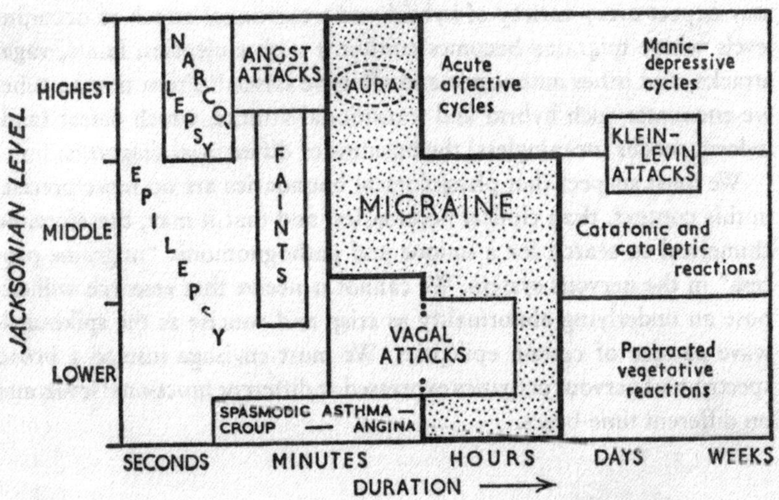

Fig. 9. Migraine in relation to some allied disorders

Migraine and neighbouring disorders are here represented in terms of time-base and neural (Jacksonian) level; either of these may be modulated—hence the metamorphoses to which migraine is prone. All of the disorders here represented are distinct and individual, but nevertheless have borderlands in which they merge into another.

THE WAITING ROOM

Charlotta Björklind

IDE ON EITHER SIDE AND YOU'LL UH, GET QUITE A SHOW, SO UH WE'LL BE ON THE GROUND IN A LITTLE

At first glance, it looks like any waiting room: chairs lined up against the walls, a couple of end tables discretely lit by dainty lamps, a potted plant, some illustrated books, and a selection of magazines for the restless to browse. Judging by its appearance, we could be at the dentist's, the realtor's, or the accountant's; however, the psychoanalyst's is unlike other waiting rooms. Those temporarily seated here have stepped out of their everyday reality. They now vigilantly wait, paused at the threshold of a completely private room that no one else can trespass. This is not simply a pragmatic description; it is an axiomatic imperative. The mother, mistress, or difficult boss might be talked about, but they are never invited in, because the aim of each fifty-minute exploration is not to ascertain whether the boss *is* a psychopath, whether the mistress *will* ever leave her partner, or whether a mother *was* inadequate. The task is to laboriously uncover one's own contradictory inner representations of these relationships, one's own conflicted motivations.

The clock counts down to the scheduled time. The appointment is circumscribed by a specific ritual directed toward the unknown and the uniquely individual—toward the staging of an inner reality whose exterior momentarily fades from view. For this reason, the atmosphere in the psychoanalyst's waiting room is frequently perceived as solemn and formal. The tension one feels differs from what a dental patient or a home buyer might experience due to the shape of uncertainty that an analysand bears, which is marked by the imprint of both desire and fear.

The walls of the waiting room are usually adorned with framed pictures, some strikingly familiar—a comforting welcome for the person who will soon be ushered into the unknown. And yet, why does this room feel odd? Seemingly innocent details signal something disturbingly unfamiliar, similar to how other homes felt as a child when sleeping over at a friend's. Why these slippers? What a strange doormat . . . It doesn't smell like home . . . Why did they hang this faded Miró poster? Similar reproductions hold the gaze of those in the waiting room, allowing their thoughts to wander. If you've ever sat outside a psychoanalyst's consulting room and felt this recurring sense of disquiet, you might recognize it as fear, not of the person you are about to meet but of your own inner transparency, which you both hope for and sincerely wish to avoid. Or, what frightens you *is* precisely the other person you are about to meet—the parts of yourself that remain incomprehensible, the impulses that overwhelm you and appear alien, even though they are your own. The transformation one expects to occur upon crossing the threshold could be described in geographic terms as a transportation—a move not only from a waiting room to a consulting room, but also from one inner space to another. In fact, the metaphor of *place* enjoys a privileged position in psychoanalytical terminology, which we'll return to later.

THE NARRATIVE SELF IN CRISIS

The human psyche constantly strives for comprehensibility, a fundamental order upon which to rely, and we have a number of tools at our disposal to help us achieve the tolerable, albeit fleeting, feeling that we are able to make some sense of our lives. In his model of the various phases in the development of a differentiated core self, psychoanalyst Daniel Stern declares the narrative self to be the most advanced stage.[1] Around the age of three, children take a developmental

1 See Daniel Stern, *The Interpersonal World of the Infant* (London: Karnac Books, 1985).

leap. Their newly established ability to name things, emotions, and desires proceeds into the realm of narration: short phrases are combined to form meaningful units, an awareness of temporal and geographic anchoring in reality is acquired, and cohesive stories with a beginning, middle, and end are created.

Representing a paradigm shift in the intersubjective matrix, this ability enables a completely new level of communication with the surrounding world. There's now the potential for sharing thoughts, fantasies, and inner reality. However, this new capacity for self-narrative inevitably alienates us, precipitating a never-ending struggle. If we borrow Lacan's metaphor of the mirror stage,[2]

2 Jacques Lacan, *Écrits* (Paris: Éditions du Seuil, 1966).

we may say that the self, in terms of the figure we experience as "ourselves," does not appear until we accept the *image* of ourselves, which is the coherent designation we perceive in the other's gaze when we realize they see us from the outside. When we understand that the other apprehends us as a separate entity and we are able to embrace their gaze, we escape—at least in some sense—the fragmented, sporadic, impulsive, inner perspective that characterizes pre-psychic or pre-intersubjective life. When we identify with the other's imagined gaze upon us, we receive an identity as a relationally mediating individual.

The ego is subsequently constructed of images and narratives, which we can reproduce and convey to people in our immediate vicinity. While presenting a coherent figure, the mutually incompatible nature of these fragments somewhat negates the longed-for experience of wholeness (which we only realize after the fact). The fragments can never be fully incorporated into the narrative flow; they pop up like buoys, surfacing in surprising places, signaling when least expected, sometimes like a slap in the face from nowhere, reminders of something archaic but ongoing within us.

In everyday life, most people regard both themselves and the world as passably coherent. We approach our existence based on the assumption that reactions, actions, and intentions are comprehensible within their contexts, that the outcomes of our choices can be understood by others. We perceive that we are ourselves over time, and to some extent, we understand how others see us because we recognize our own emotional states and attitudes. Still, confrontations with the incomprehensible are inescapable. Life throws us into crises, sometimes activated by external changes—moving house, a divorce, an infatuation—other times appearing as if from out of the blue. We develop symptoms in the form of unpredictable anxiety, depression, or psychosomatic micro eruptions—unwelcome surprises from our inner world. These confrontations are rarely pleasant, often painful, and sometimes downright frightening. What is this thing inside me that does not figure in my narrative or everyday self-understanding but which I suspect is me?

G AGO. I FLY TO SAN FRANCISCO IN THE MIDDLE OF THE DAY AND RETURN TO LA AS NIGHT FALLS. I'

CAN THE BODY SPEAK?

A schematic diagram by neurologist Oliver Sacks of migraine in relation to some allied neurological disorders illustrates the human desire to understand and map our experiences and shortcomings in order to make sense of our lives. Using the phenomenology of neurology, Sacks sought to explore our experience of migraine conditions by assessing them in terms of duration and intensity. While he included the subjective sphere of experience, he did not deviate from the medical paradigm's desire to map and distinguish, explain connections and differences, in order to predict and prescribe remedies. Nevertheless, Sacks realized that, while separate and individual, neurological disorders have "borderlands in which they merge into another," which incidentally recalls the perpetual and futile attempts of psychiatry to demarcate and distinguish between different pathological mental disorders. Psychiatry, as a medical subspeciality, strives to map mentally unhealthy and healthy "conditions" based on the assumption that they are analogous to somatic disorders. From a philosophical or existential point of view, this seems insufficient. Needless to say, the issue has been debated for hundreds of years. What does it mean to experience oneself as known and unknown, as functioning and suffering, as being alive?

The dispute may partly be explained by the fact that the abilities we use in trying to understand ourselves are contingent upon and anchored in the body's actual organs. The organs we use to view the function of an organ are one in the same. *How does it work?* We are constantly concerned with this question. How is our individual concrete existence in external reality, i.e., the world, translated into an inner experience? How is the body's materiality linked to inner psychic reality—to how we experience ourselves? And what do we make of the fact that our conscious experiences are so full of gaps and contradictions? We live in the tear of an interface. The incomprehensible becomes especially tangible when we are ill and experiencing symptoms, when our body/soul deviates from the homeostatic condition characterized by the expression "good health is quiet." If migraine rears its ugly head as soon as I go on holiday, if anxiety descends when I'm about to indulge in something particularly desired, or if melancholy intrudes on a celebration, we sense a context for questioning and brush up against the realization that *it doesn't make sense.* The mystery of the nervous system's causal link to inner life remains unsolved. Neither neurology nor psychology can provide a scientifically comprehensive answer. Some specific abilities may be localized to focal activity in the cortex or subcortical structures, but consciousness still eludes us. Despite its phenomenological palpability, consciousness is not physically present anywhere. Yet, it appears to be everywhere—in the brain, the nervous system, the total corporal internal mass-communication between neurons. Consciousness is a totality that emerges from and yet exceeds the sum of its parts.

As it so often does, psychoanalysis introduces a paradox in order to relate to the question of the body's connection to the mind. Jorge Canestri called this scientific-philosophical point of departure psychoanalysis' *dual aspect monism*[3]

[3] Cf. Cartesian dualism and the naive monism of somatics.

HAUSTED. I HAVE A DEEP FATIGUE THAT NO AMOUNT OF SLEEP CAN HELP. YET ALL I WANNA DO IS SLEEP

and referred to Sigmund Freud's postulate that the drive impulse (fundamentally a psychic phenomenon) is not equivalent to biological instinct.[4] The psyche is

4 Jorge Canestri, "The Complexity of the Dialogue Between Neurosciences and Psychoanalysis," (European Psychoanalytical Federation Symposium: Psychoanalysis in 2025, Berlin, 19–21 September 2014).

not composed of physiological processes; it presses against them in an indeterminate relationship of intimacy. While physical stimulus is the source of the drive impulse, fantasy instantly arises in the psyche in the wake of a stimulus that is idiosyncratic and arbitrary, even though it is completely dependent on the original stimulus. Fantasy is not a simple representation of a physical correlate; rather, it is an immediate, albeit intricately complicated, end-product of multi-stage symbolic condensations and displacements, in which metonymic movement, via intimacy links, gradually washes out the first impulse's radicality through numerous changes of context. Again, we may notice that the conscious thoughts we eventually join together in our narratives have been transformed beyond recognition, even though they bear traces of their origin. It's for such reasons that no two migraines are exactly alike, even though they are activated in the same areas of the brain.

GEOGRAPHY AS METAPHOR

No matter how far medical science advances, we will never be able to conclusively measure or map any individual's experience of being. To describe our unique somatopsychic reality, we resort to metaphoric language. Lisa Tan offers us the opportunity to read Oliver Sacks's phenomenological migraine diagram as a floor plan. Through association, she metaphorically relates inner experiences to spatial imagery, aligning with psychoanalysis's frequent use of geographic metaphors. Freud referred to his first model of the mental apparatus as topographical and illustrated it with an image that looks very much like a map. The unconscious id is portrayed as a vast, obscure area at the bottom; the preconscious is located higher up, above the transversal brickwork of censorship; and perception and our (according to the diagram, very small) conscious ego are placed at the apex, looking very much like an eye. Two decades later, Freud presented his famous formulation, "the ego is first and foremost a body-ego,"[5]

5 Sigmund Freud, *The Ego and the Id*, trans. Joan Riviere (London: Hogarth Press and Institute of Psycho-Analysis, 1927), 31.

to describe how the child's rudimentary sense of an autonomous self initially derives from bodily sensations.

Again, we must remind ourselves that these somatic impressions do not constitute a self—they are sprawling, incoherent, and contradictory. The self does not appear until the next phase, when we begin to identify with the (other's) image of us or with the narrative of ourselves. The factual, objective body cannot be fully represented, and even if the ego emerges from the bodily experience, it is also inevitably alienated from it. Our subjectivity derives from this alienation in relation to the body and its concrete reality, and to describe the psyche as the collected, organized experience of somatically grounded perceptions and sensations is, consequently, a fundamental misunderstanding. The map of our inner world is *always* a metaphor; we cannot use it to navigate, in a concrete sense. At the same time, we seem intuitively to experience our interior world as a landscape; we spontaneously speak about different inner places. Freud invites the reader to imagine Rome not as a geographic space but as a human psyche through which he guides us.[6] Donald Meltzer claims that psychoanalysis should

6 See Sigmund Freud, *Das Unbehagen in der Kultur* [Civilization and Its Discontents] (Vienna: Internationaler Psychoanalytischer Verlag, 1930).

set out from the psyche's so-called geographic aspects, where the psychoanalytical work is understood as an organization of "geographical confusions."[7]

7 Donald Meltzer, *The Psychoanalytical Process* (London: The Harris Meltzer Trust, 1967).

Countless psychoanalysts have written about the experience of the mother's body as the child's first exploration of the world and its geography. Map metaphors attempt to lend an impression of uniformity but, despite their prevalence, never fully succeed in capturing the human psyche. Remainders that cannot be incorporated into the narrative persist—disturbing elements that make themselves known as holes in the weave of meaning, gaps in comprehensibility. For the psychoanalyst, these blank spots on the map provide clues for uncovering that which is hidden and repressed. The point of departure is the unconscious—not just the parts that are momentarily inaccessible or subtly implicit, but also those regions that are actively withheld, forbidden, and incompatible, which we nevertheless carry around.

DREAMS AND ART AS SECONDARY PROCESSES

In a letter to his close friend Wilhelm Fliess,[8] Freud jokingly muses whether

8 Sigmund Freud and Wilhelm Fliess, *The Complete Letters of Sigmund Freud to Wilhelm Fliess 1887–1904*, trans. and ed. Jeffrey Moussaieff Masson (Cambridge, MA: Harvard University Press, 1985), 417.

a marble plaque will be placed on the house where he had stayed five years earlier in 1895 and where he began work on his book *The Interpretation of Dreams* (1899). It was there that he analyzed his own dream of "Irma's injection,"[9]

9 Sigmund Freud, *Die Traumdeutung* [The Interpretation of Dreams] (Leipzig & Vienna: Franz Deuticke, 1900).

which would become pivotal to his concept of the universal dynamics of the psyche. This was not a sudden revelation; it had been preceded by a decade's worth of meticulous and intense work via hypnosis, theories of the explosive power of traumatic memories, and suppositions of the structuring function of repression. By submitting himself to systematic self-analysis through deconstructing his own dreams, Freud was able to arrive at the groundbreaking insight that dreams, just like symptoms, are not rooted in repressed memories of horrible experiences but reveal hidden secrets: forbidden desires and aspects incompatible with our conscious (and desired) coherent self-understanding. The dream we remember when we wake is the result of secondary processing: consciousness's narrative-creating function that cobbles together fragments to make intelligible stories. Upon awakening and before censoring and secondary processing have begun, there is, according to Freud, raw material in a latent dream, which has managed to disguise through condensation and displacement the original, unconscious, and for the dreamer, forbidden impulses in a symbolic form. With the knowledge of how these primary processes work, Freud imagined that we'd be able to decode the final artifact and, by interpretation, arrive at our hidden secrets because they are simultaneously concealed and communicated by dreams. The unconscious works on this transformation by means of what Freud called the *dream-work.*

Freud declared that dreams should be regarded as the psyche's fundamental paradigm, the pattern for all the contents of the unconscious. Everything from neurotic symptoms, jokes, slips of the tongue, and inexplicable forgetfulness to a culture's artistic expressions and religious worldviews can be regarded and approached as if they were dreams. Freud hoped this would enable us to deal with impressions, work through the distortions of censorship, and convert the contents of the unconscious into an intelligible language. (Un)fortunately these hopes did not come to pass. Freud suspected that we would never be able to fully reveal that which is latent. He called this inscrutable core *the navel of dreams.* Not only is the unconscious inexhaustible, it is unrepresentable. Its fragments belong to another paradigm that is constant in the human being, and as long as we live, they will continue to disturb—and sometimes threaten to completely destroy—contexts we have so laboriously constructed. At the same time, there's an opening here. Psychoanalyst Wilfred Bion used the term *negative capability*, first introduced by the poet John Keats, to describe our crucial but only potential ability to bear uncertainty.[10] If we believe that we already know,

10 Wilfred R. Bion, *Attention and Interpretation* (London: Tavistock Publications, 1970).

entrances will remain closed. If we set out to determine the specific meaning of a particular symbol, we will deprive ourselves of all its meanings. The symbol can never be possessed by one specific meaning, because then it will lose all its symbolic qualities and fail to communicate anything. We have to let it be free, allow it to shake us up, and then dare to let it go so that next time something else will be activated. We can never step into the same river twice. This is, of course, where art comes in, with its potential to simultaneously represent the totality and its protruding, noncontiguous fragments, which may point to or stir up something in our inner world without directly referring to it. We may be reminded of something we have experienced, or something desired or fantasized about may be revealed, but often it is implicit—we are touched or shaken without really knowing why. These loose fragments constitute signs for an individual; they don't point to an exact meaning but link to a network of deeply private connotations that are both unconscious and mobile. Art is similar to crises in the sense that it may cast us out of the narrative and into a connection with something we may be unprepared to face but which we, at the same time, recognize. Such experiences are paradoxically the reason why one may find herself in a psychoanalyst's waiting room.

Y INTELLECT CAN'T KEEP UP WITH WHAT TOUCHES ME. I WORK TOO MUCH BUT SO DO A LOT OF PEOPLE. I

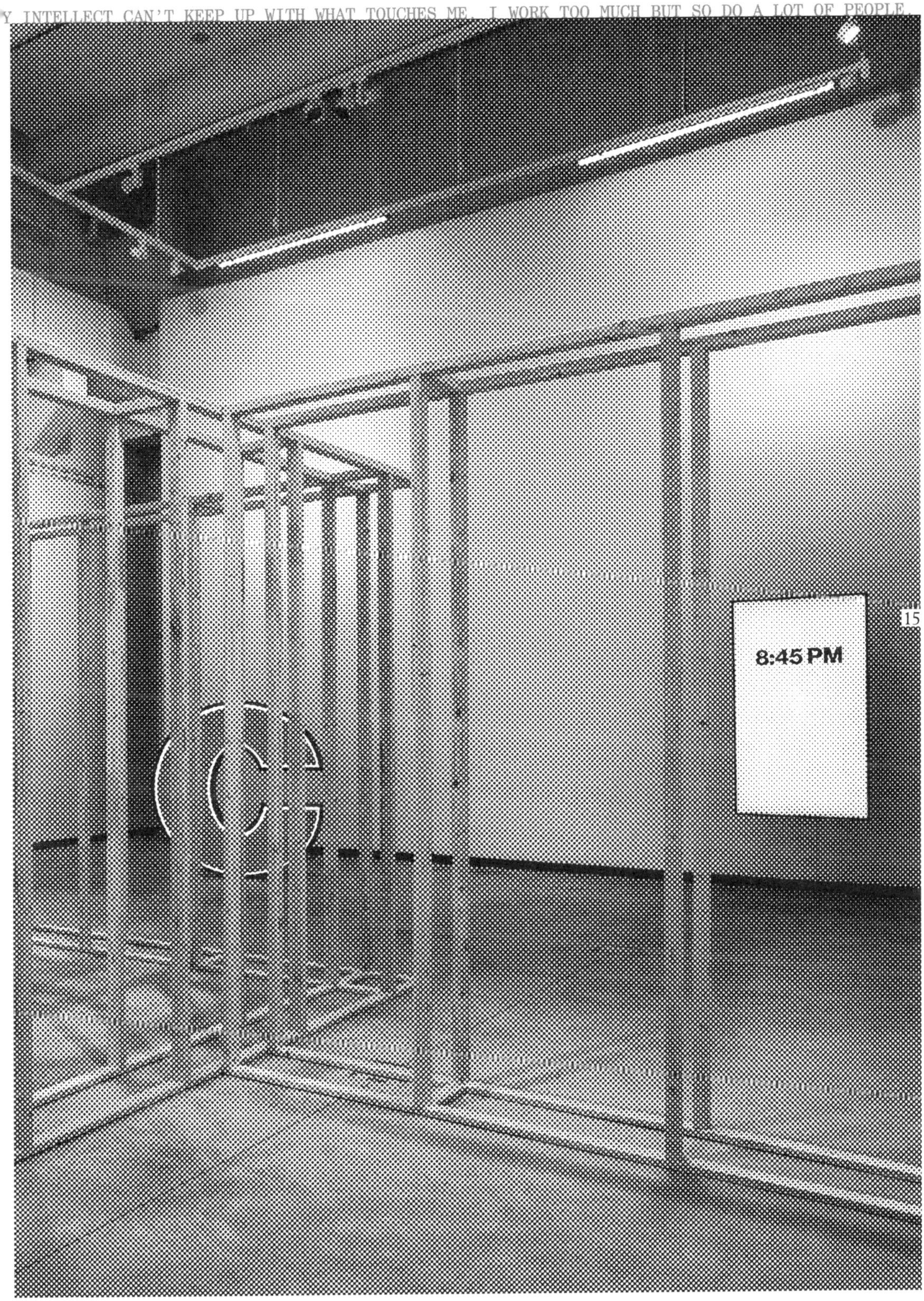

T FIREWORKS MAKE AS THEY LAUNCH OR THE LOW RUMBLE WHEN THEY EXPLODE. I ONLY HEARD THE PLANE

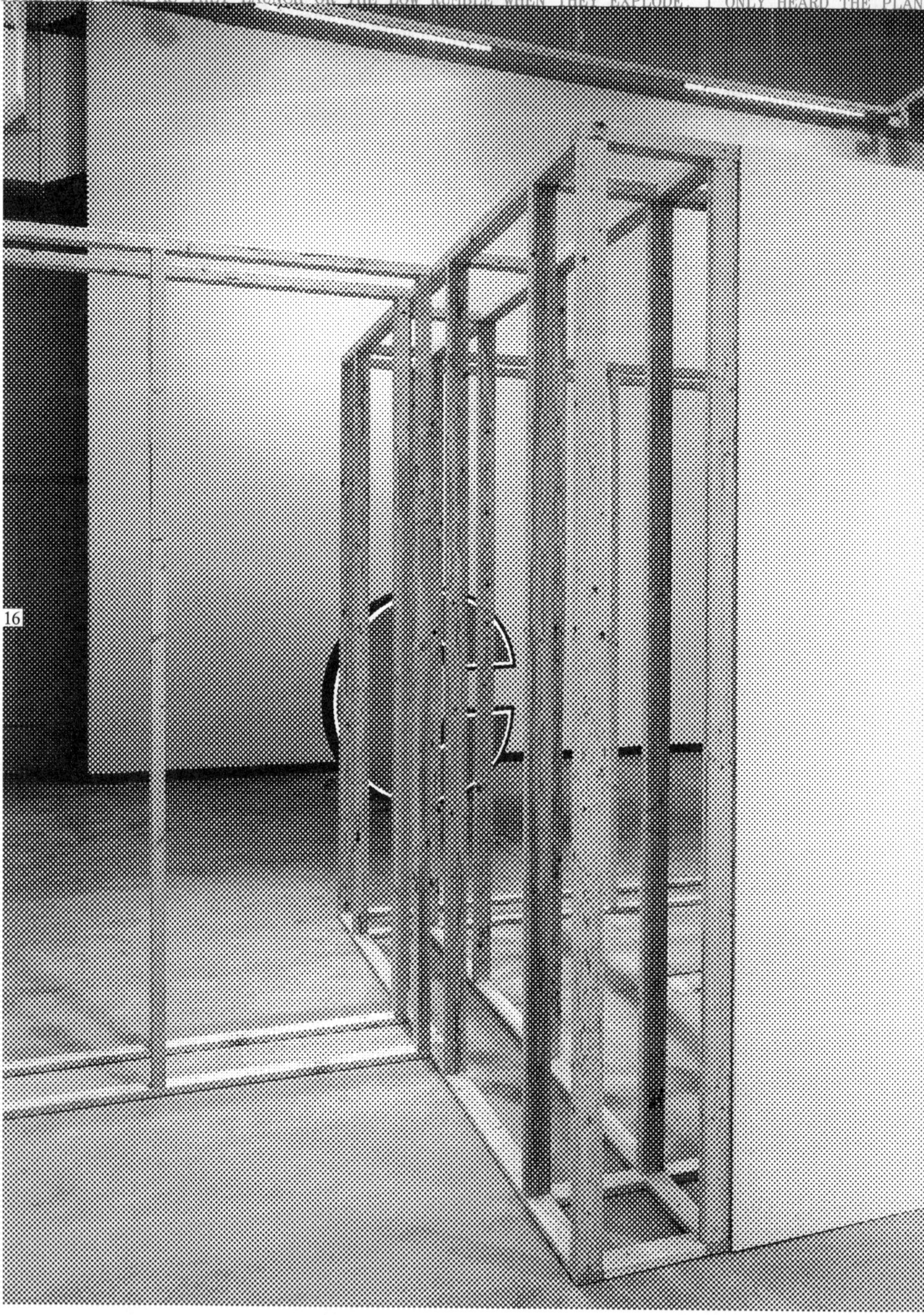

TION SYSTEM AS IF IT WAS CIRCULATING SOMETHING DARKER. I DECIDED WHEN AND IF IT MADE SENSE

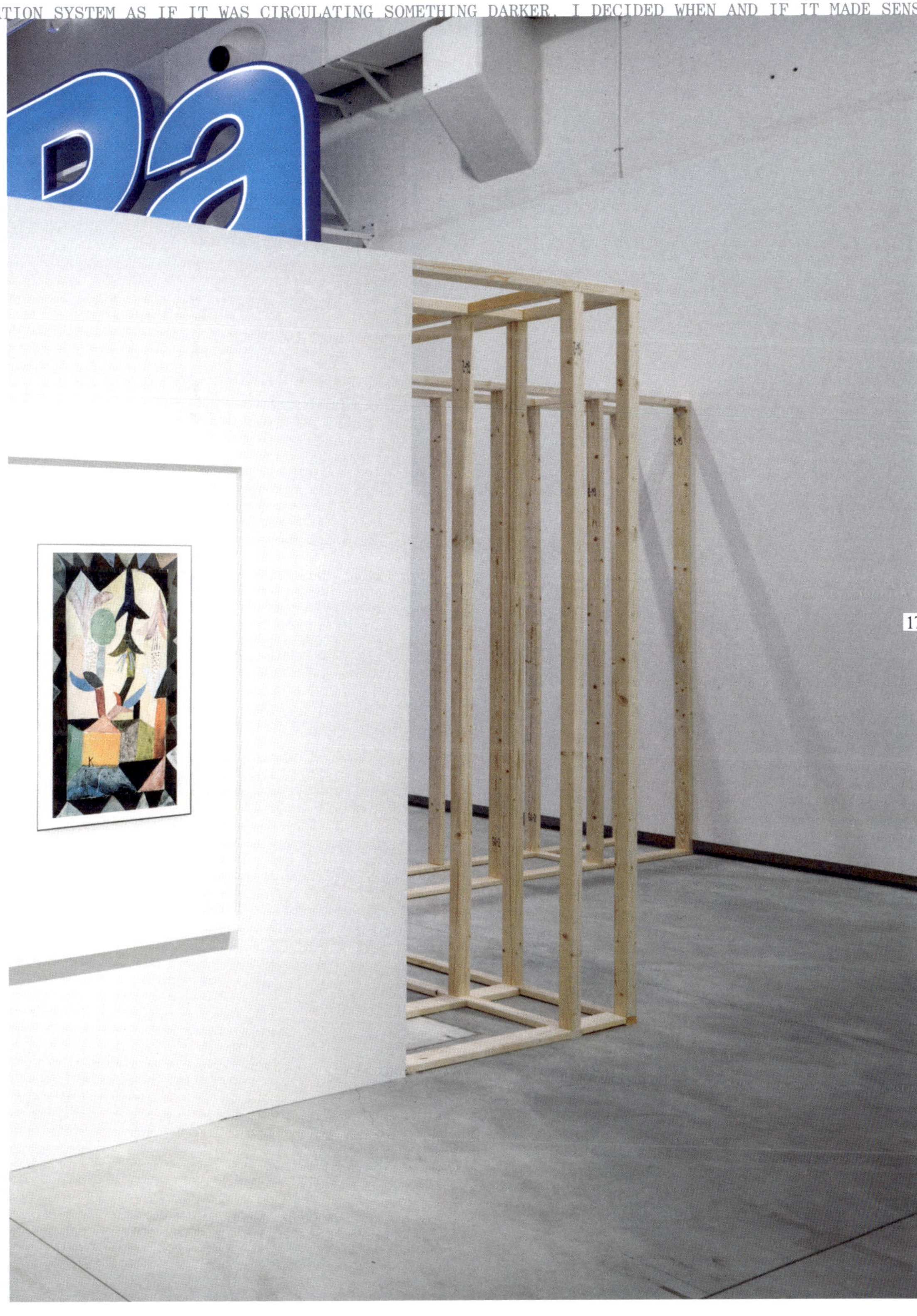

IGHT. I WAITED. AND COME THE SUMMER OF TWO-THOUSAND SEVENTEEN FOLLOWING THE US ELECTION OF

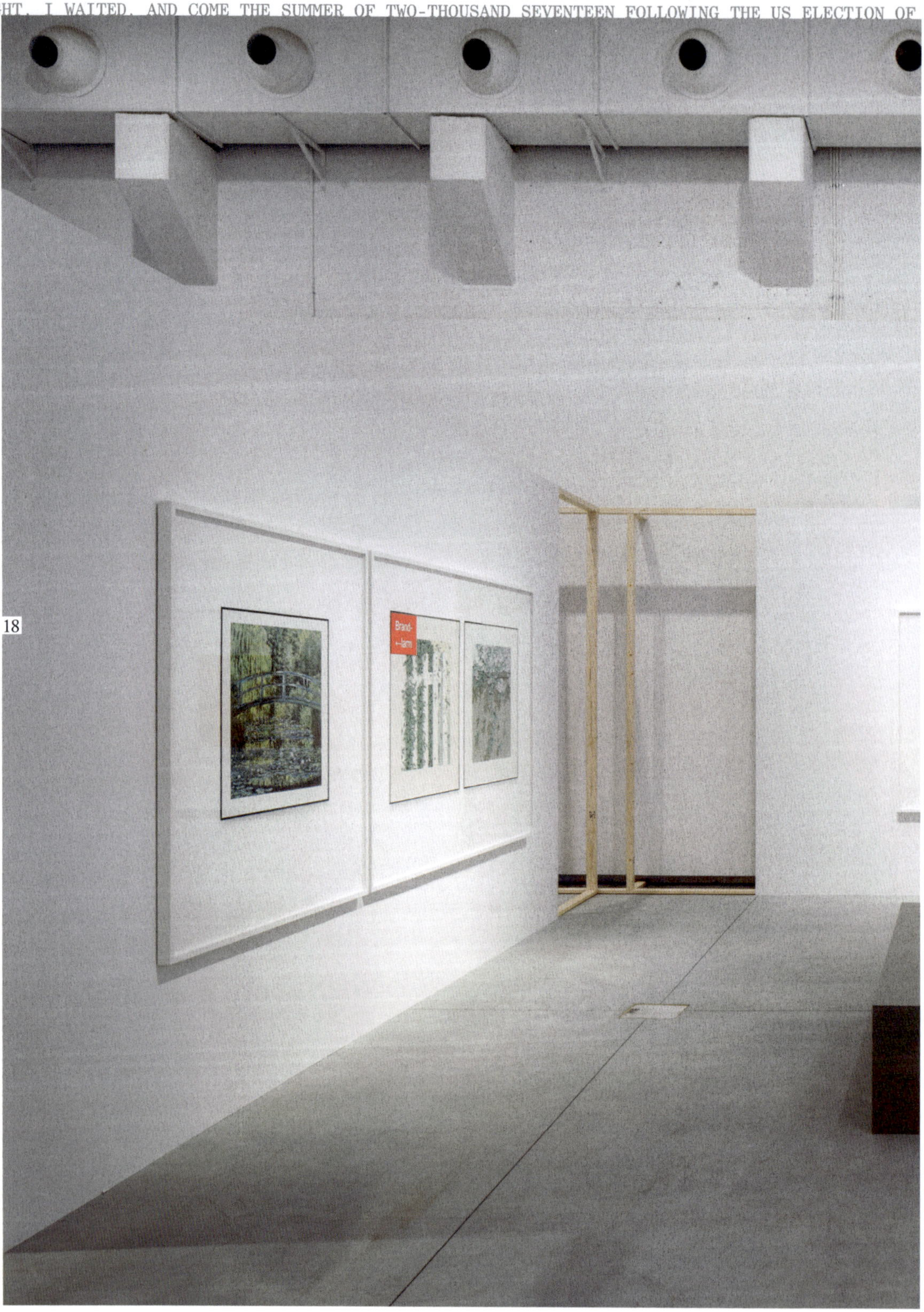

AND SIXTEEN. IT WAS TIME BUT I REALIZED IT TOO LATE AND WOULD HAVE TO WAIT ANOTHER YEAR. I'V

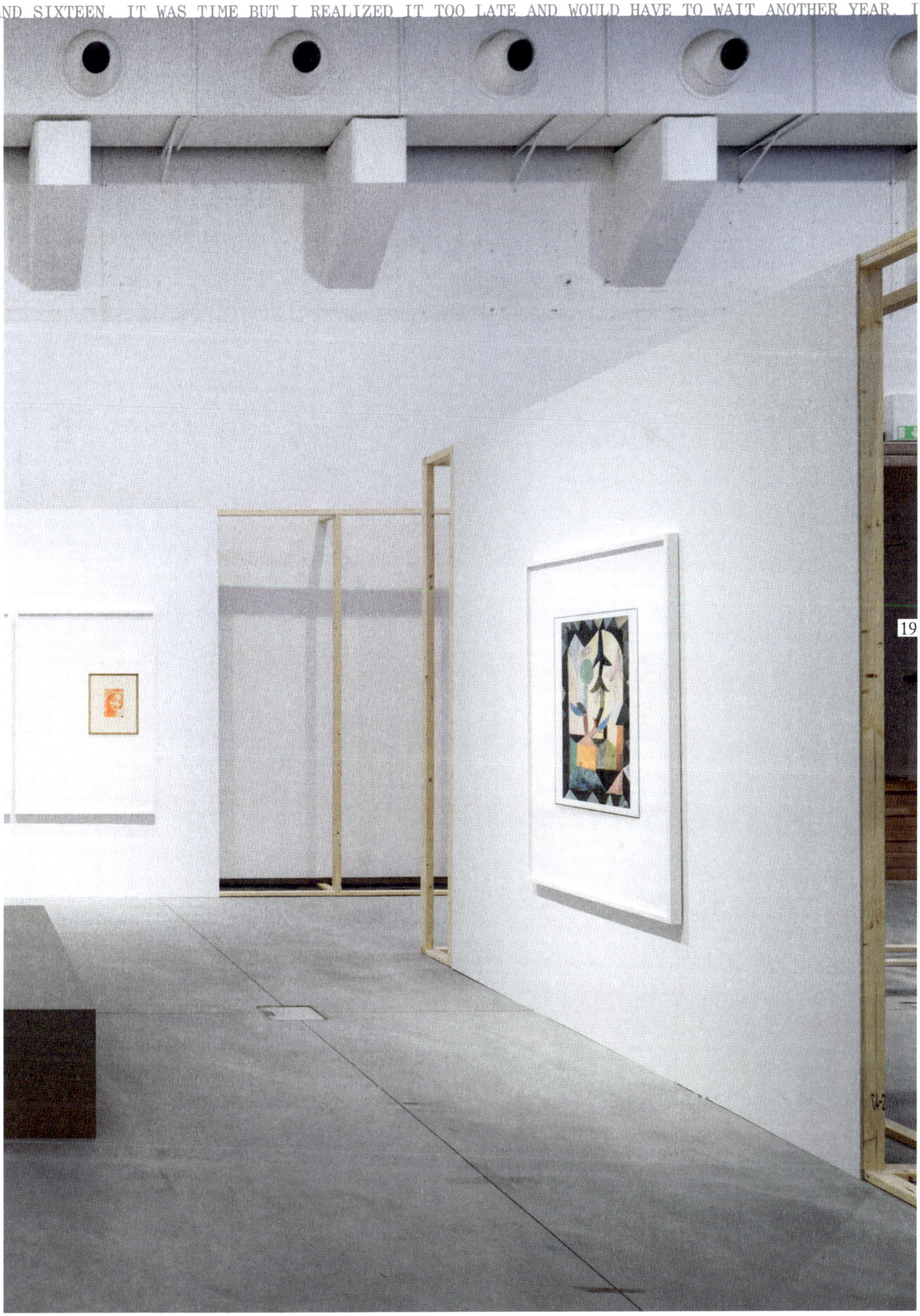

TURN TO FILM THE SCENE. I KNEW THAT I WANTED THE IMAGE TO BE RECORDED FROM A COMMERCIAL AI

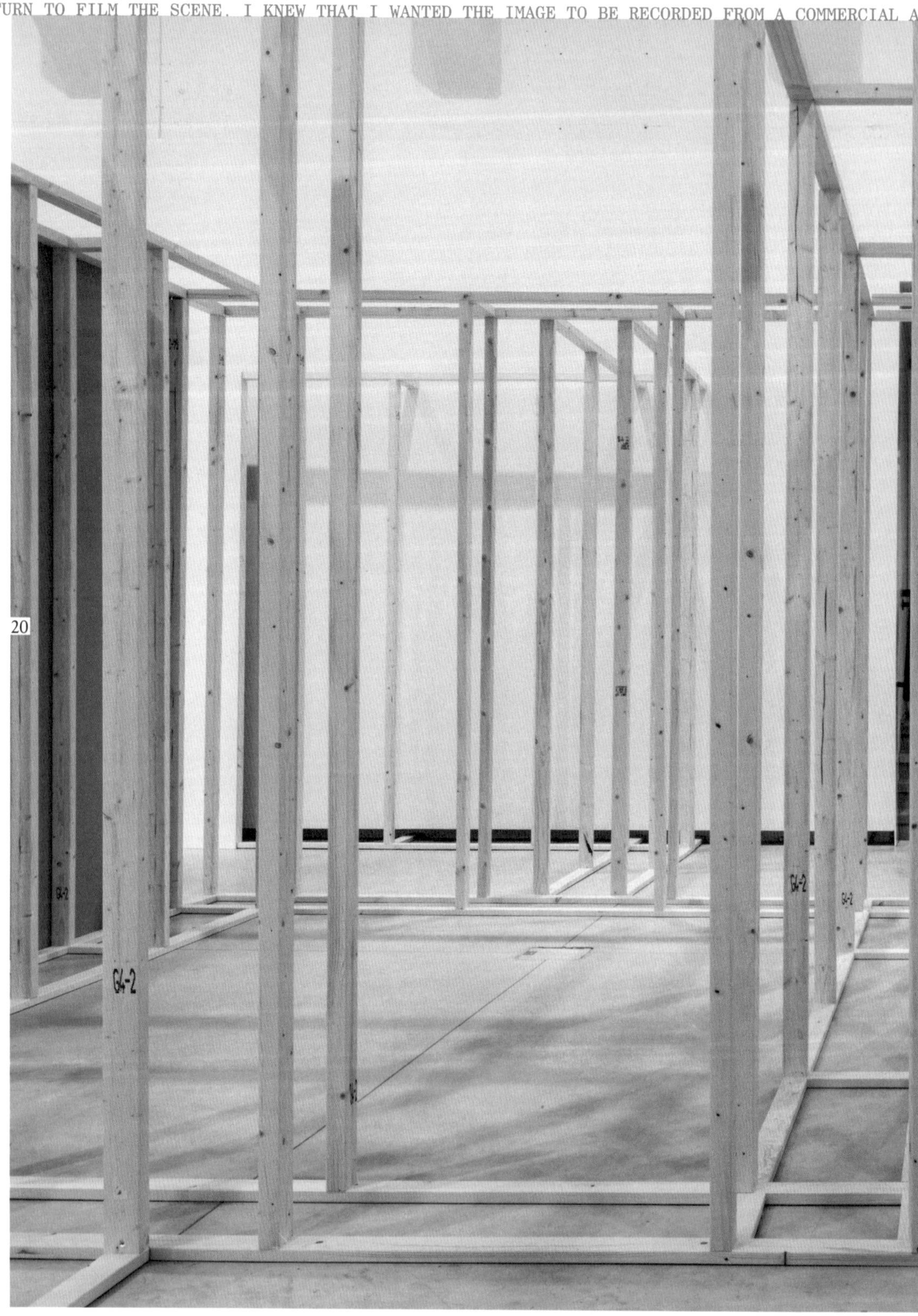

OT FROM A HIRED HELICOPTER. NOT WITH A DRONE. BUT IN THE SEAT OF ROUTINE EVERYDAY COMMERCIA

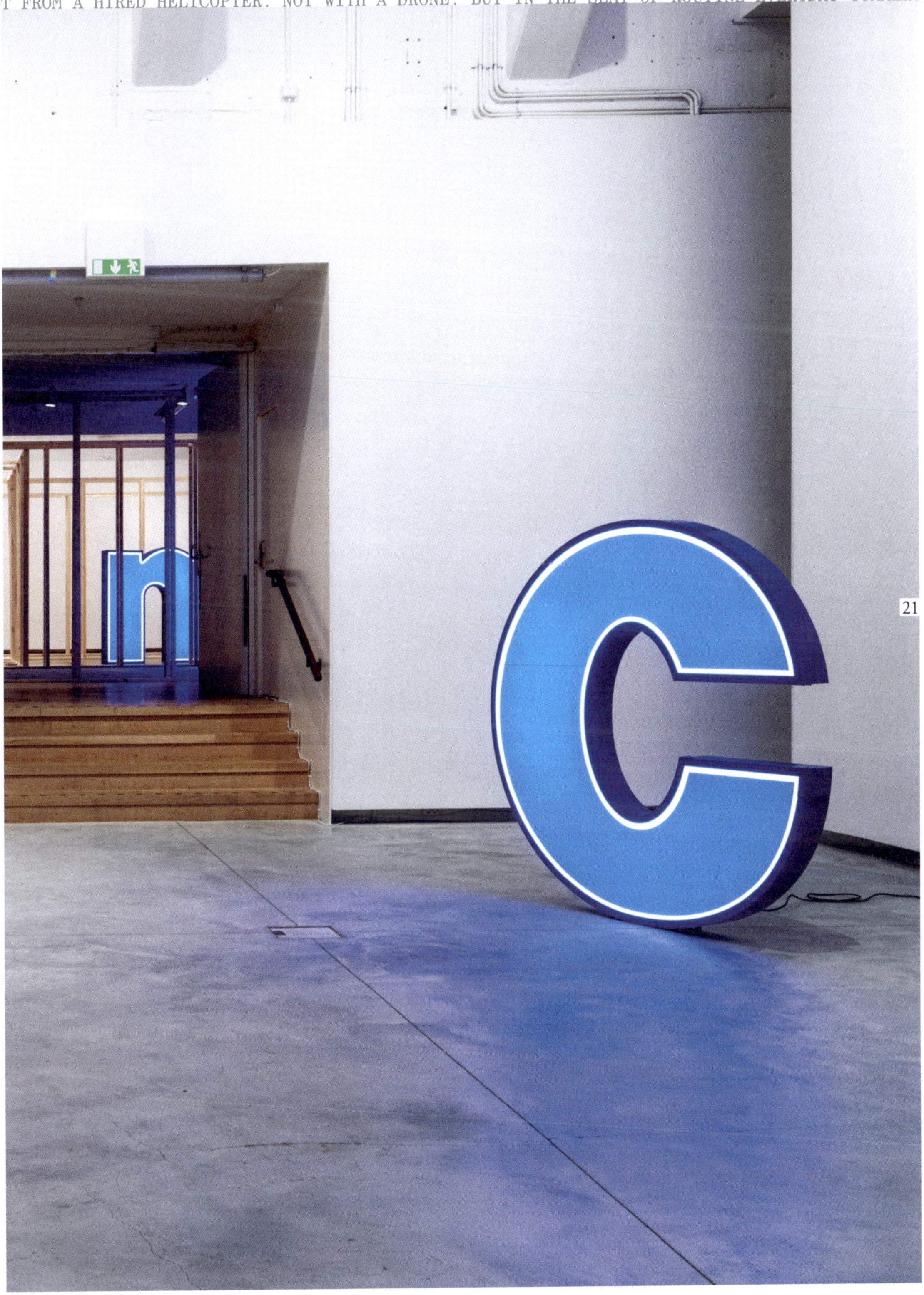

TRIED TO FILM THE SCENE FOR THREE CONSECUTIVE YEARS, AND EACH TIME, I HAVE FAILED TO GET T

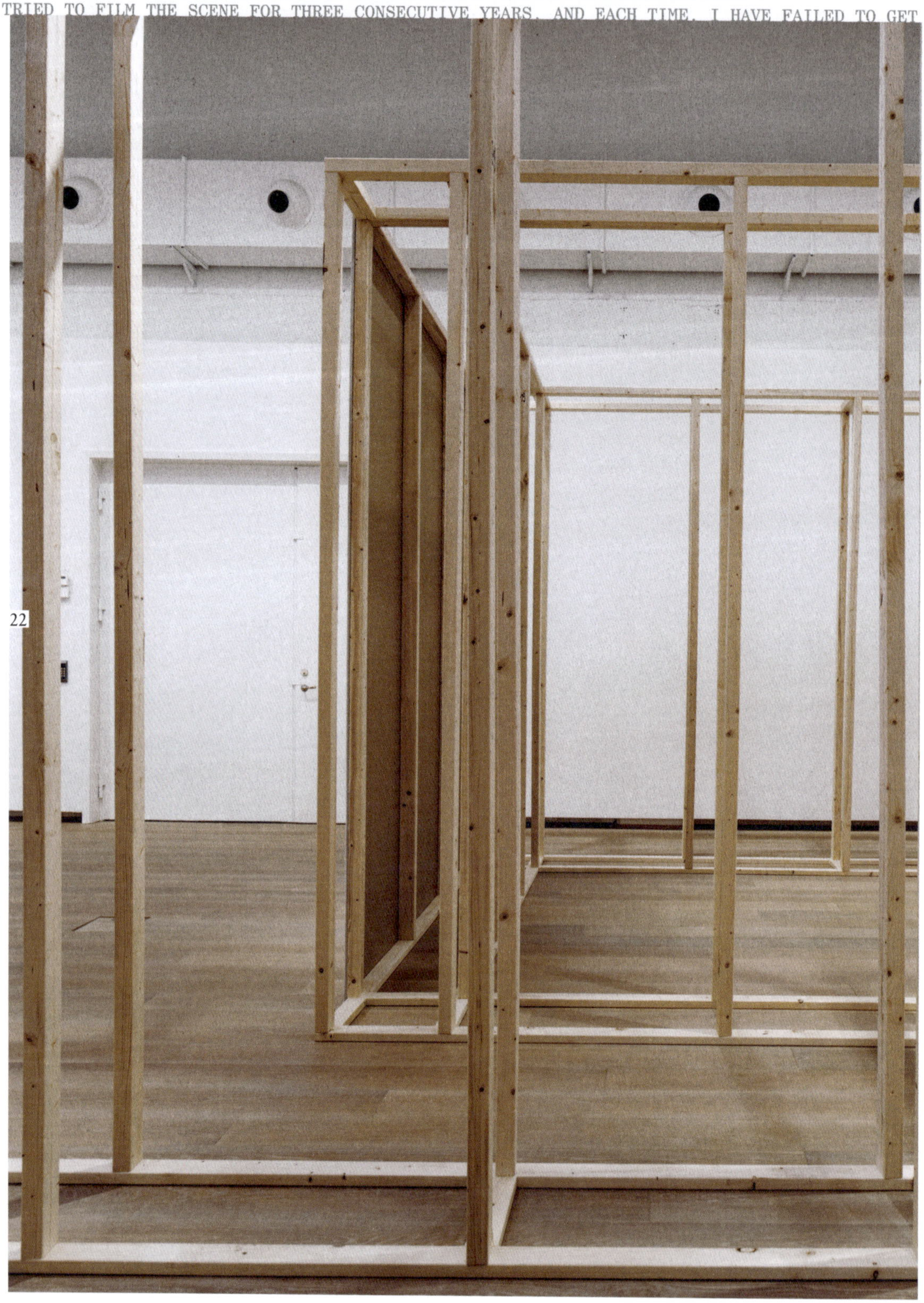

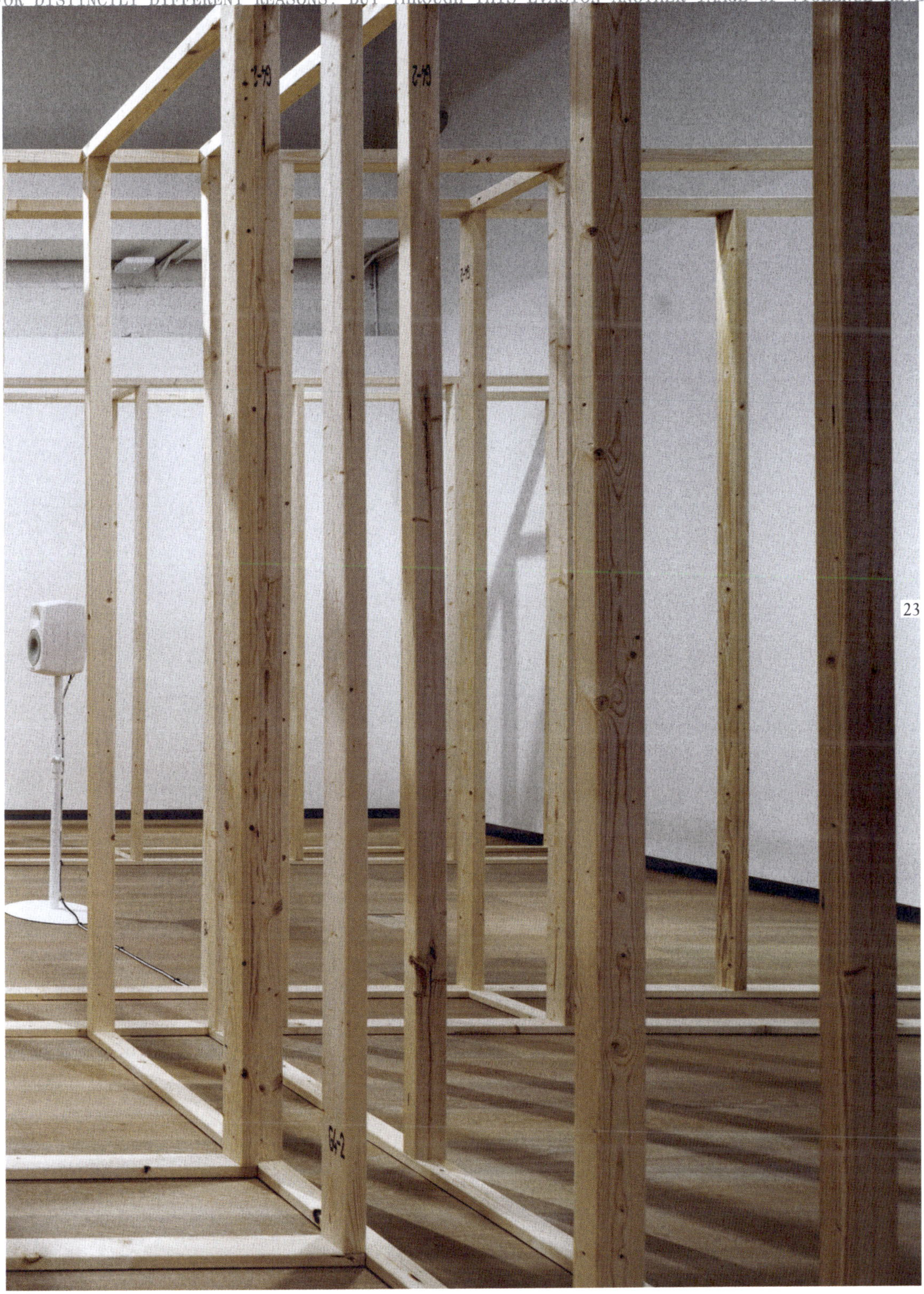
Z-49
Z-49
G4-2

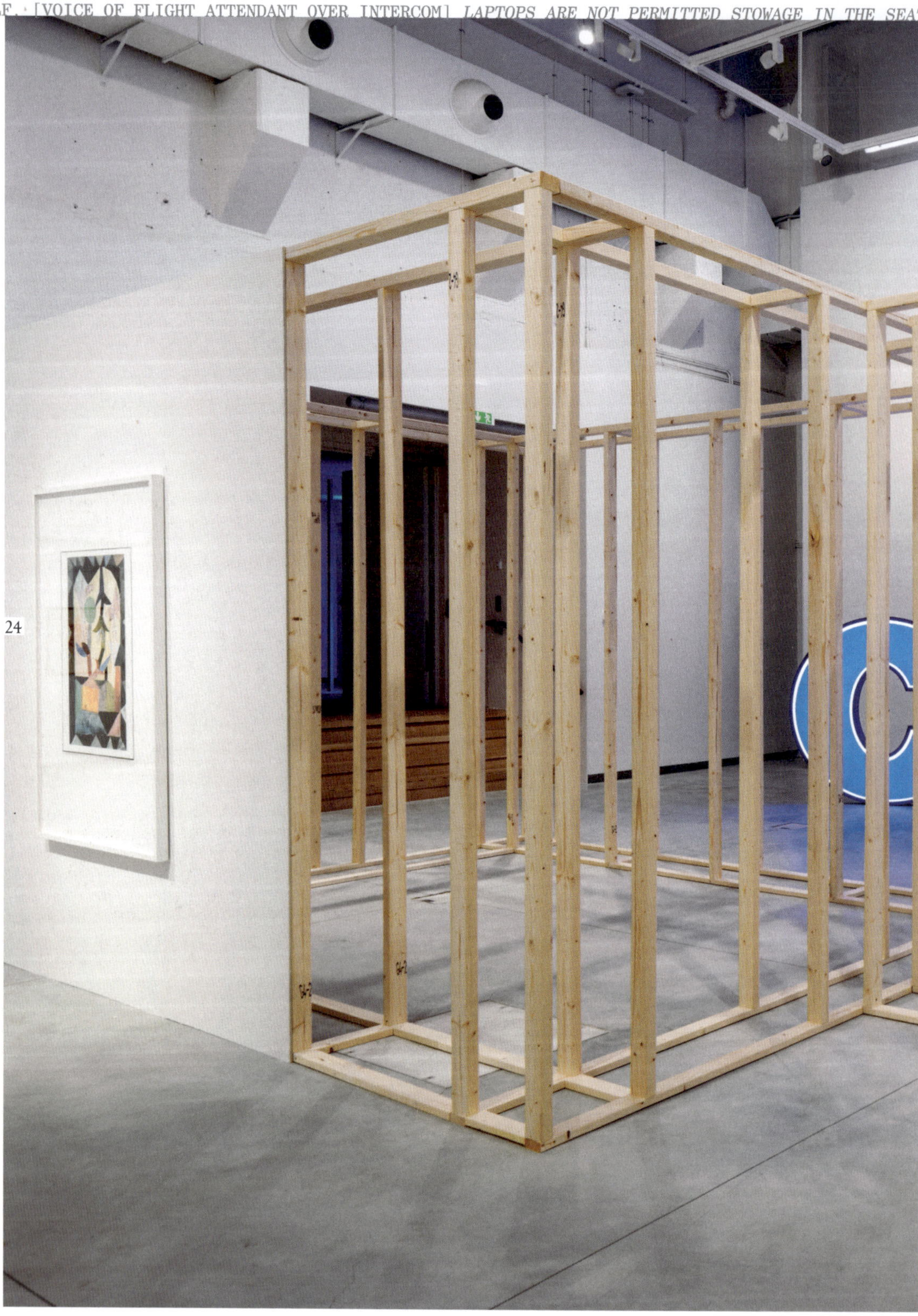

ETS. PLEASE WE'LL BE COMING THROUGH THE CABIN TO COLLECT ANY LAST MINUTE RUBBISH ITEMS INCLUD

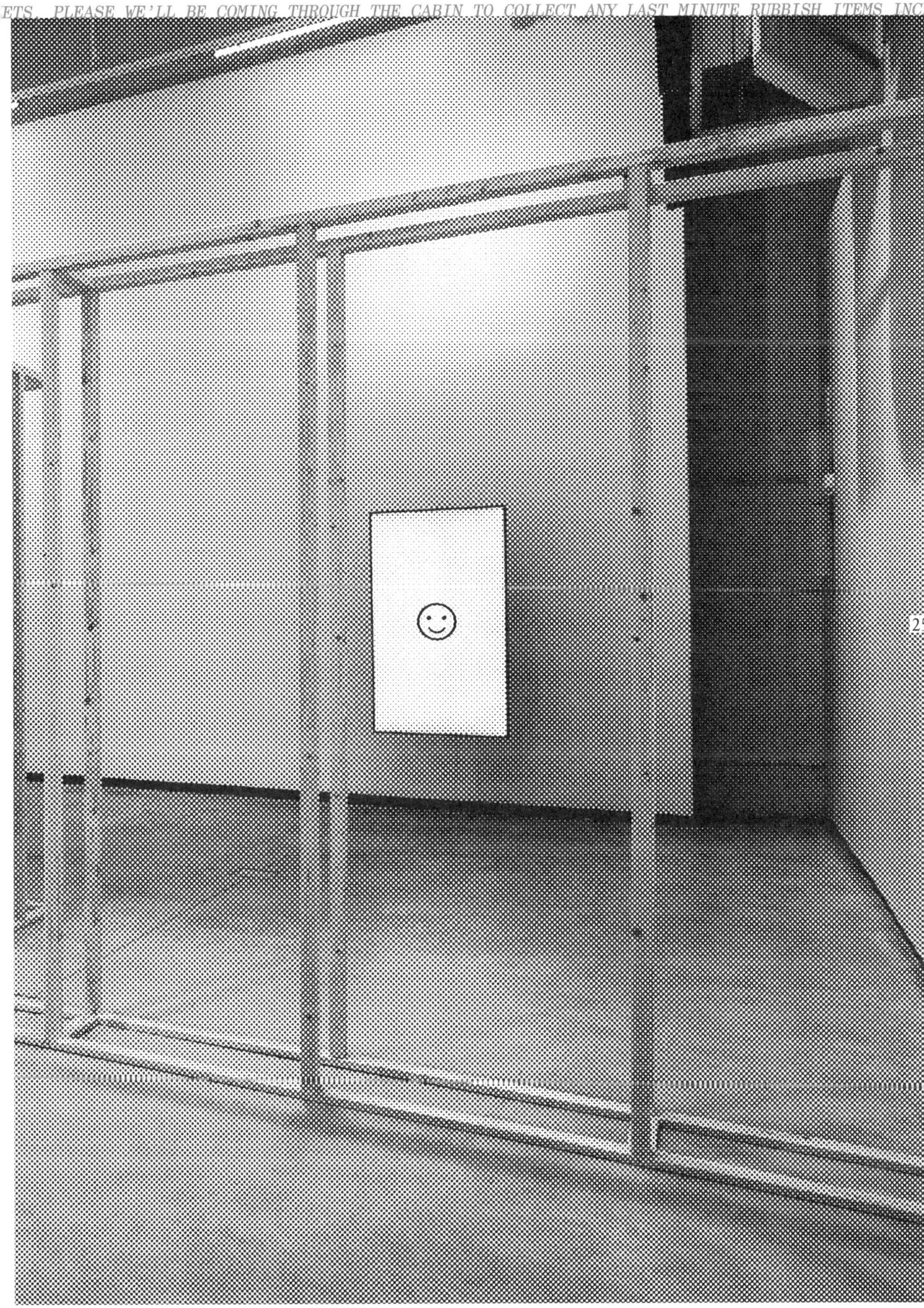

LIFT

26

Asier Mendizabal

RUNWAY, UNTIL IT'S TIME TO MAKE A FULL U-TURN. AND PLANES FROM THE EAST MAINTAIN AN ELEGANT,

INNER VOICE

Of all the sources we might choose from when identifying with the narrator's voice in any given story, the most disconcerting is the one that compels us to imagine its words are our own thoughts; that such words aspire to our own concatenation of ideas, arising within our mind while we read or listen to them; that the stream of consciousness of the source thus speaking is fully naturalized in our brain's interior, so that the emerging ideas appear to constitute our own thinking. Listening to (or reading) a voice that comes not from a character but rather from an indeterminate narrator forces us to consider two equally illusory choices: locating it in the narrator's consciousness or in our own. Without the mediation of a character who speaks it, the effect such narration produces is either that of listening to it resonate in the mind of another or making it resonate inside our own, that of temporarily inhabiting a foreign consciousness or letting ourselves be inhabited by it. The images and metaphors with which we imagine the mind are, almost invariably, spatial. Spatial metaphors are, almost invariably, images of limits, thresholds, and borders.

The effect of identifying with a narrator's thought process perhaps seem so natural to us because it replicates the way in which what we call inner voice takes place. Inner voice refers to a mode of thinking formulated in our mind as a finished discourse consisting of articulated and completed statements that we would tell ourselves, as though vocalizing, inside our heads, the phonemes that embody ideas. The dissociation suggested by this is fascinating because if our own brain is responsible for making thoughts emerge and for establishing connections among them, why would the mediation of an entirely articulated language imitating a voice and an ear be necessary? Who utters and who listens to this interior monologue, which, as we know, amounts to only a small fraction of our, for the most part, automatic and inarticulate cognitive activity? So natural does the organization of thought as language seem, that we tend to minimize the singularity of those thoughts that appear as speech insofar as they produce the acoustic illusion of being heard. Those moments when we want to record a memory, encourage or issue ourselves an order, those when we rehearse what we wish to verbalize next; or those when we, frustrated, elaborate too late that which we would have wanted to say on time . . . are concrete cases where the mind seems to duplicate, making thought resonate in the spatial interval created by a conversation's two poles.[1] Daydreaming is perhaps closest to the idea of a fiction nar- 1
rated by a voice, at once actor and audience, in our mind's scenario. Bachelard's *poetics of space* locates daydreaming in wandering—through rooms and corridors—relating every inner story with an inner architecture, imagining consciousness as a theater or as a house. A favorable space, anyhow, for acoustic resonance.

The cinematographic convention—forever revealing in its naive narrative resources—guarantees that, while listening to a voice-over, we perceive the difference between the narrator's discourse and a character's inner speech. When we hear the voice of an interior monologue apparently outside the story's diegesis, but distinct from that of an omniscient narrator, this voice resounds with a more or less evident *reverb* effect. It is as though the echo defines an enclosed space where the voice of consciousness rebounds, conferring a moral mandate, a regret, or a

IT LINE. DURING THE FINAL DECENT, ALL ARRIVING FLIGHTS QUEUE DIRECTLY ABOVE NEIGHBORHOODS W

repressed thought with cunning gravity. Where else are we invited into, if not the literal interior of the head belonging to the character who thus thinks? In what walls or vaults would it resonate other than in those of a mind contained
2 in the bony architecture of a cranium?[2]

VOICE-OVER

Lisa Tan organizes *Dodge and/or Burn* with a spatial proposal based on lifting—as though it were a blueprint—a diagram drawn by Oliver Sacks that explains the different stages of migraine and other neighboring disorders. Interpreting the diagram—which defines different stages of pain—as a map corresponding to the areas of the brain where the disorders are located would be a mistake, of which Tan herself warns us. The diagram is a representation of intensities and durations, of passages between stages and their respective limits and thresholds, rather than a map pretending to locate these conditions. But it is impossible *not* to see the diagram as a blueprint where the chambers, living rooms, and hallways of an inner architecture are distributed and where the person who suffers from migraine pain (and Lisa herself has always suffered from it) moves from room to room. The diagram inevitably suggests the passages between different intensities and variables of pain as a wandering inside the mind, imagined as a living space, a house.

 As she overlaps the lines of Sacks's diagram with those of the exhibition room, Tan generates a disjointed double space, a paradoxical overlapping of two realities that evokes—such is the thinking that guides my writing—the duplication between brain and mind. In *Dodge and/or Burn*, Tan's own voice, resonating across the room, is what unifies both overlapped spaces: the one created by the temporary grid lifting Sacks's diagram and the one formed by the architecture holding it. The voice spills over and resonates throughout the rooms and passageways we traverse, until we find its source in the video *Dodge and Burn*, a title paraphrased in the exhibition's own. In the video, the narrator's voice-over associates the bumpy development of a repeatedly attempted, but never quite fulfilled, film project with a series of personal confessions derived from the project's process itself. The burnout, frustration, and doubt that characterize the contemporary artist's role resonate with the political conditions of existence, manifested in the United States' tense political situation at the time of filming. The story of an unfinished film project starts to become the film itself, unfolding as we listen. The diction, slow cadence, and tendency toward a controlled
3 low pitch bestow upon the voice the authority of a narrator,[3] although the story's tone and content might be received as confessional and, thus, as deriving from a character. Such is the tension conditioning the experience of this exhibition. We are denied the condescending temptation to understand the author as a
4 character; instead, we are forced to confront the dilemma of locating her voice.[4] Are we inside the mind of the person who speaks? Is the person who speaks inside our mind?

Does that split correspond with the overlapping of the two imagined spaces? It might seem so. Three exhibition elements are set up on the original gallery

E MILITARIZATION OF THE POLICE WAS ACTIVELY DEVELOPED. A REACTION TO THE PUBLIC GATHERINGS

walls, that is, on the existing architecture. Two large illuminated letters are fixed
at a considerable height, forming the beginning of the word *Panasonic*, from which
the remaining letters, dispersed across the entire room, appear to have absconded.
Fixed in a similar way and synchronized to the story we continuously hear
resonating through the space, a vertical screen occasionally displays isolated words
with a minimal degree of meaning, primarily initials and acronyms. These are
signs appealing to a language in dissolution, or to its as-yet unarticulated poten-
tial. The third element is a set of nine framed letters. Following a regular annual
interval, these were written by Mark G. Bamberger, whose name appears in the
letterhead and signature. Tan's medical reports, which is what these letters are,
seem slightly more sympathetic and intimate as the years go by, but they never
deviate from the self-contained tone of cordiality and authority expected from
a doctor's voice. Upon silently reading the letters—while imagining the Doctor's
voice or substituting it with our own[5]—the sound of authority surely reverber- 5
ates as an extremely polite command from the superego ("Everything would
be better if you could better control your stress"; "I suggest somehow finding time
to resume your previous exercise or yoga routine"). But, beyond that, there is
a revelatory inversion in these letters. Whereas the obsolete epistolary form was
primarily used for the purpose of recounting to a recipient how the sender felt,
in these letters, the sender's voice relays to the recipient her own state of health,
replicating the game of lodged, projected, and adopted utterances suggested
by the voice resonating across the space.

IZENS IN 1965, WHO WERE ORGANIZING AGAINST HOUSING DISCRIMINATION AND POLICE VIOLENCE. FOUR

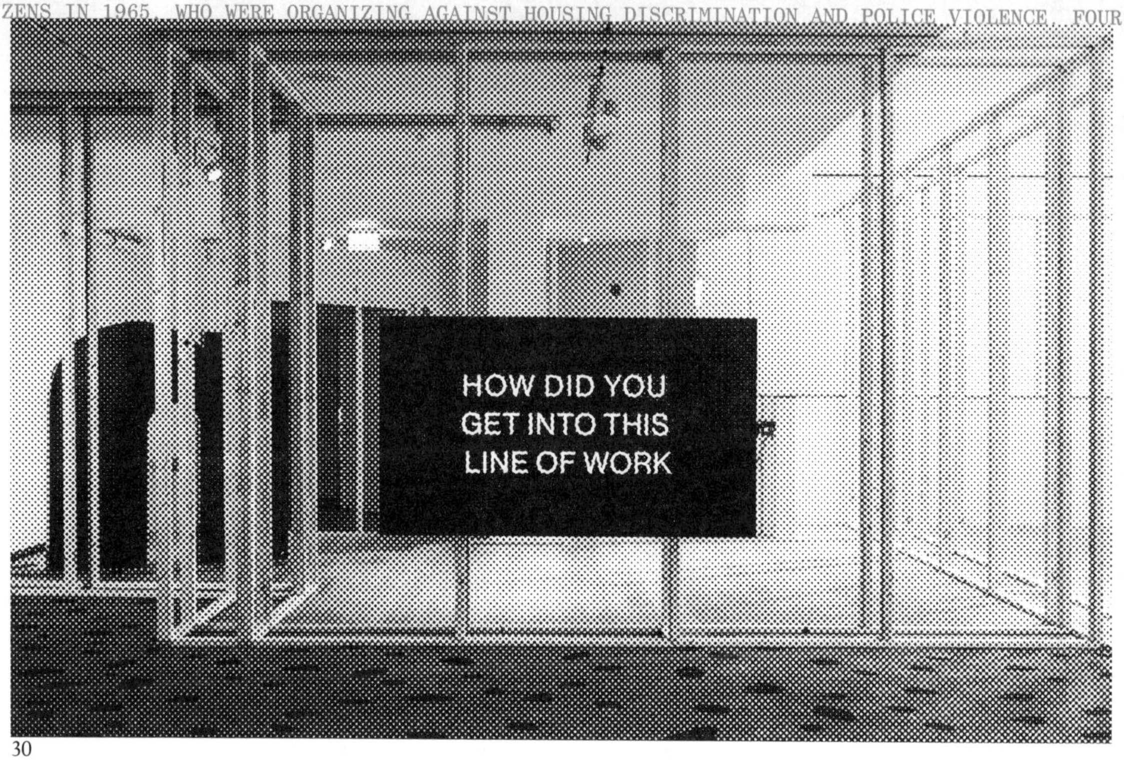

TER. THE VERY FIRST SWAT TEAM WAS DEPLOYED FOR A RAID ON THE BLACK PANTHER PARTY. AS MY FLIG

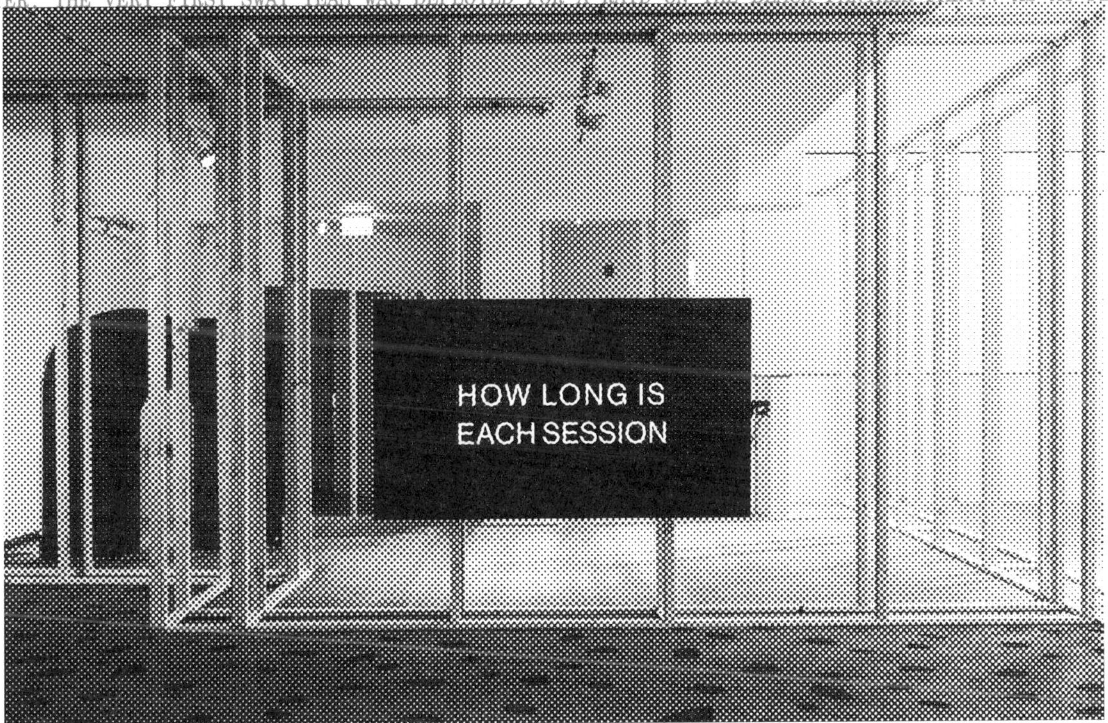

RESONANCE

The series of works located in the other architecture, on the provisional walls replicating Sacks's diagram, also evoke the relationship between patient and authority. Between patience and authority. Each of two chambers replicate waiting rooms, where reproductions of artworks—some more generic than others—hang as one would expect to find them in the reception of a doctor's office. I am tempted to associate these waiting areas with one of the inner voice cases enumerated above: the instances when we recite in our consciousness something we want to be sure of verbalizing. As though rehearsing a role, we resonate in our mind what shall be said before proffering a consequential declaration, a confession, an account of symptoms. Language's insufficient mediation is seldom felt as intensely as when we find ourselves in this place of impatient waiting, going over what we should or should not say, or when we find ourselves traversing this place in bafflement, attempting to articulate what we should have said but didn't, because we forgot or because it is only now that the precise idea occurs to us. In every clinical exercise, the difference between the sign and the symptom is that of a state's objective expression (a bruise, an inflammation) and its subjective manifestation mediated by language. The idea that pain is perceived not in the site of the actual harm itself but rather as a representation in our brain would be an echo of said difference. Such forms of specular representation, which we can only express through utterance, always leave us with incapacitating doubt as to language's adequacy and a resigned acceptance of its insufficiency.

After all, the idea that there is a dissociation between what we feel and how we can translate it into language replicates the neurocognitive paradigm, according to which the brain is a map of connections functioning as though it were a mirror for what the body feels: "Common sense tells us that our pains are in a physical space within our bodies, that for example, a pain in the foot is literally inside the area of the foot. But we now know that is false. The brain forms a body image, and pains, like all bodily sensations, are parts of the body image. The pain-in-the-foot is literally in the physical space of the brain." However, Thomas Fuchs, from whose *Ecology of the Brain* I am quoting, rebuts: "The brain does not feel pains, nor does it contain them. It does not produce a 'body image' either, for the experienced body is not an image of a body, it is rather the body itself as felt." Following this argument, the paradox proposed by migraine would be evocative, as the place where the pain is felt is the same space where it is decoded. Do we not encounter here a paradoxical overlapping of two spaces like *Dodge and/or Burn*'s two planes? If diminishing consciousness to mere neural activity seemed to dispel the metaphors of the mind as an inner space where our thoughts resonate, it seems odd that neurology's main form of knowledge production would be locating each activity in its respective brain zone, each pain on the map of the encephalon's various areas. And it is almost poetic—however tendentious this reasoning may be—that the medium through which neurology performs such zonal localization on the brain's anatomy would be magnetic *resonance* imaging, what MRI stands for.

The uttered word, even in the inner voice's imagined, silent echo, is different from the thought, from the idea, from the unrealized potential suggested by the neural network's image. 33

The waiting rooms simulated in the exhibition correspond to those of a psychologist and a neurologist.

THRESHOLDS

Migraine has a characteristic visual manifestation in particularly painful stages. Generically called aura, it appears as a blot that blurs or blocks part of the patient's vision. Despite being a blinding phenomenon, it was visually represented as *scintillating scotoma* by Hubert Airy in 1870, who depicted it in terms of military architecture: "In its height it seemed like a fortified town with bastions all around it." Airy describes with words what he visually shows in his treatise, a zigzagging line which, indeed, looks like a wall: "All the interior of the fortification, so to speak, was boiling and rolling about in a most wonderful manner as if it was some thick liquid all alive."[6] A fortification is not a house, and I am 6
forcing the associations here as I bring up this visual metaphor with which to speak of walls, limits, and borders. However, I cannot *not* perform the comparison. Oliver Sacks's migraine diagram is not, as we have said, a spatial map in the way an architectural plan is. It cannot be—and this is a detail we do not immediately realize—because if the areas demarcated in the drawing were rooms, they would have doors. There are no openings between these spaces, which obfuscates the type of relation presumed to exist between the stages of pain. If the relation is not that of a passage between rooms, then it can only be one of liminality, of contiguity, represented in those lines without doors, those lines as thresholds. In psychology, the threshold is the minimum degree of stimulus that human

sensory organs are capable of perceiving. If neuroscience's popularized imaginary dictates that consciousness takes place in the interval between neurons ("You are your synapses!"), in the passage formed by discontinuity, then a more evocative figuration of mental activity derives from imagining thresholds rather than doors.

According to a suggestive etymology, the word *door* in Latin languages—from which English retains *portal* or *port*—comes from an ancient Roman ritual performed to mark the foundation of a city. "The ritual consisted in plowing the limits of the future settlement, elevating the agricultural instrument on the segments destined to become sites of entrance and exit. From the verb 'portare,' in its link with the gesture of elevating the plow on those cavities, . . . the noun
7 'porta' would have derived."[7] The door is, in the ritual's suggested inversion, the limit's discontinuity, and the threshold is the limit itself, of which the door is the exception. The consciousness of a limit is already that of its overcoming; the awareness of a frontier, that of its crossing. The door is nothing more than the point where such spillover condenses. Given philosophy of language's dictum that the limits of my language mean the limits of my world, the threshold we are driven to transcend between our interior and the world is that of utterance. That of uttering what-is-not-yet-world since it is still only thought. That which becomes world only when we manage to enunciate it. The membranes emitting and receiving the voice are, at once, limit and door, and only through vibration
 and resonance can they make a word concrete. In *Waves*, a video produced by Lisa Tan in 2015, we hear her voice-over, her serene and firm narration, thinking these words aloud: "Speaking of limits, philosophers have said that the limit is comprised of affects and that even though they are tricky to fully describe, it's only language that can keep their something else-ness afloat, long enough for us to see what we can describe."

Endnotes

1

Mladen Dolar identifies these as the typical instances when the inner voice resonates. His *A Voice and Nothing More* attends to the particularity of that voice without sound and its connection with word and meaning. I cannot help but include this footnote with the sole purpose of quoting the following image from his book: "Beyond the voice 'with flesh and bones' (as Jakobson will say some decades later) lies the fleshless and boneless entity defined purely by its function—*the silent sound, the soundless voice*." Mladen Dolar, *A Voice and Nothing More* (Cambridge MA: MIT Press, 2006), 17.

2

Suddenly intrigued by the technical aspect of this effect, I visit an online forum for sound engineers, where I find the following exchange:
@Utopia: Hi, I'm currently working on a short film in which a character is often talking inside his own head. I just wondered if anyone had any tips on creating an effect on the dialogue in which it feels enclosed and gives the impression you're listening to a person's thoughts. Thanks.
@Ian: Completely dry with extra bass and a fair amount of compression, it should sound gentle and very close.
@Adam: I agree with @Ian that this works for a POV shot as it simulates the effects of bone conduction (otherwise known as "do I really sound like that?"). But for any other shot, IMHO this

GELES WE LOOK FORWARD TO SEEING YOU AGAIN SOON GOOD NIGHT [VOICE OF PILOT OVER INTERCOM] . .

treatment doesn't make sense without adding an obvious reverb that's very different from the normal dialogue 'verb. This effectively lets the audience know that we're "hearing" the thoughts in a different non-physical space—the mind. See any movie with a telepath for reference. *Sound Design Stack Exchange Forum*, https://sound.stackexchange.com/questions/10237/audio-effect-of-a-person-talking-inside-their-head, accessed September 21, 2023.

3

In her essay "The Gender of Sound," Anne Carson associates the patriarchal rejection of the high-pitched feminine voice with its presumed opposite, the self-restrained voice, an important feature of the masculine virtue of *sophrosyne* or self-control. Aristotle, Carson reminds us, in his effort to account for "the gender of sound physiognomically . . . ends up ascribing the lower pitch of the male voice to the tension placed on a man's vocal chords by his testicles functioning as loom weights." Apparently, the skull is not the only cavity modulating the imagined resonance. See Anne Carson, "The Gender of Sound," in *Glass, Irony and God* (New York: New Directions, 1995), 119.

4

In *The Acoustic Mirror*, Kaja Silverman shows that "Hollywood's soundtrack is engendered through a complex system of displacements which locate the male voice at the point of apparent textual origin, while establishing the diegetic containment of the female voice." The non-diegetic voice-over, that of a narrator, for instance, is expected to be male, while the voice-over of a woman will always be clearly located, embodied, in a diegetic character. Even when the voice-over corresponds with the resounding inner monologue we have discussed above, the plot manages to clearly situate such disembodied speech as a narrative necessity, typically by restaging the "talking cure," where a female character performs the out-loud thinking for the authority of an analyst, but sometimes forcing the diegetic reason for the utterance a little too far. In *Possessed*, for instance, "an unconscious woman is injected with a drug which induces her to speak on command. What she is obliged to produce in this way is, of course, her past, which flashes onto the screen as her voice embarks upon its regressive journey. Interiority is thus extracted through an action upon the body: liquid is injected into a woman in order that a cluster of memories can then be projected both onto the doctor's diagnostic 'screen' and onto our cinematic screen." (A bunch of examples in Silverman's account are from characters called Lisa or Liza . . . What's up with that?) See Kaja Silverman, *The Acoustic Mirror: The Female Voice in Psychoanalysis and Cinema* (Bloomington: Indiana University Press, 1988), 45, 59.

5

Fittingly, Kaja Silverman describes the resource of reading a letter to oneself as a particular case of "disembodied voice-over . . . both corporealized and diegeticized," when she makes the following, rather exaggerated, claim: "The only disembodied female voice-over that I have been able to find in the history of Hollywood film is that which narrates Joseph Manckiewicz's *Letter to Three Wives*." Silverman, *The Acoustic Mirror*, 48–49.

6

Hubert Airy's quotes are included in Brian Dillon's *Affinities*, where he accounts for his own experience with migraine, adding his name to an illustrious list of writers who suffered from it and attempted to describe it with words. The book also includes the referred diagram's illustration. Words rarely suffice.

7

I confess to having included this quote almost solely for pleasure of relaying its source: Anna Adell's book *De paseo por los limbos*. From that same book, and by way of an evocative image, I bring to bear here another consideration about limits and thresholds: "Before frontiers were lines, 'neutral strips' [*bandas neutras*] separated territories." Anna Adell, *De paseo por los limbos* (Wunderkammer: Girona, 2022), 113–114.

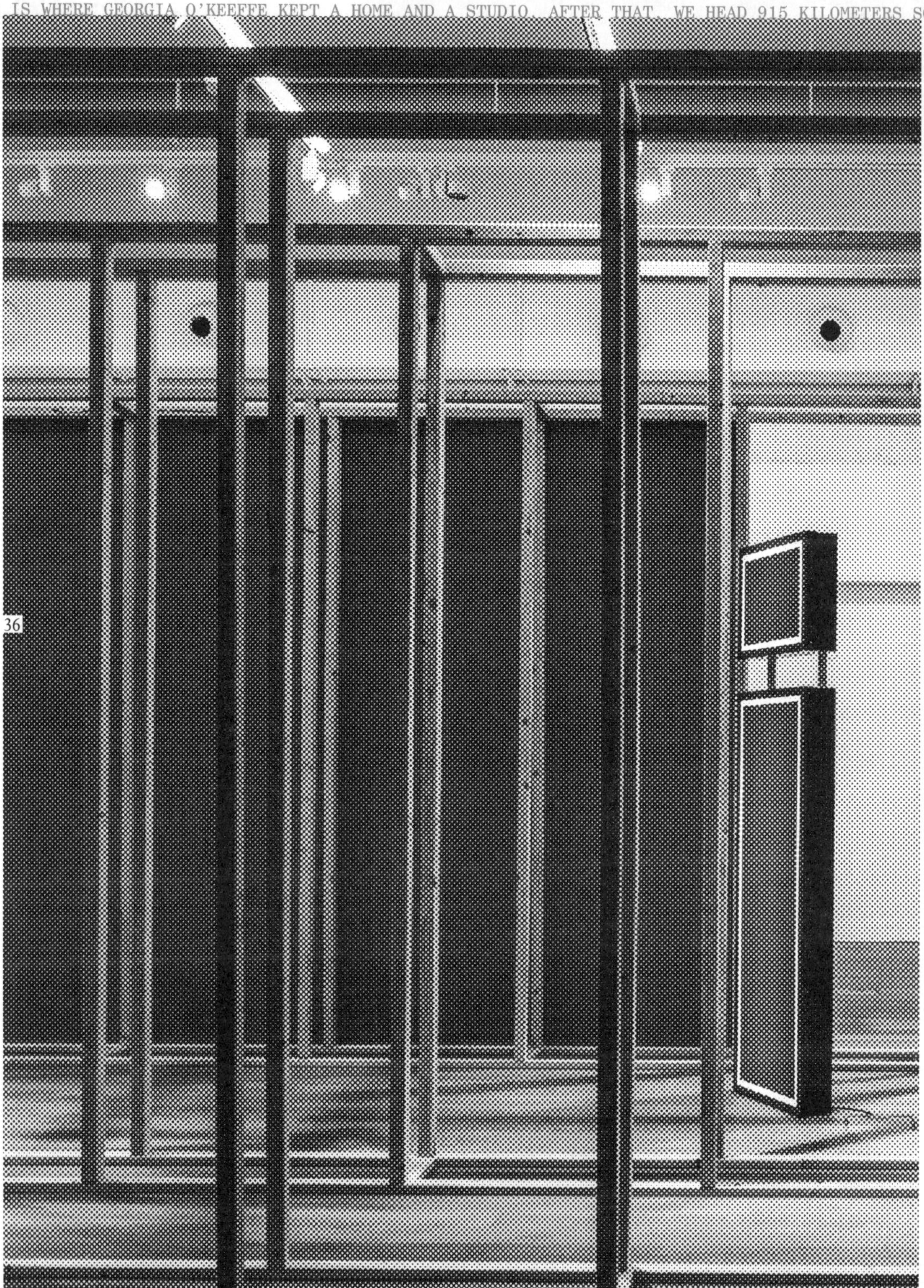

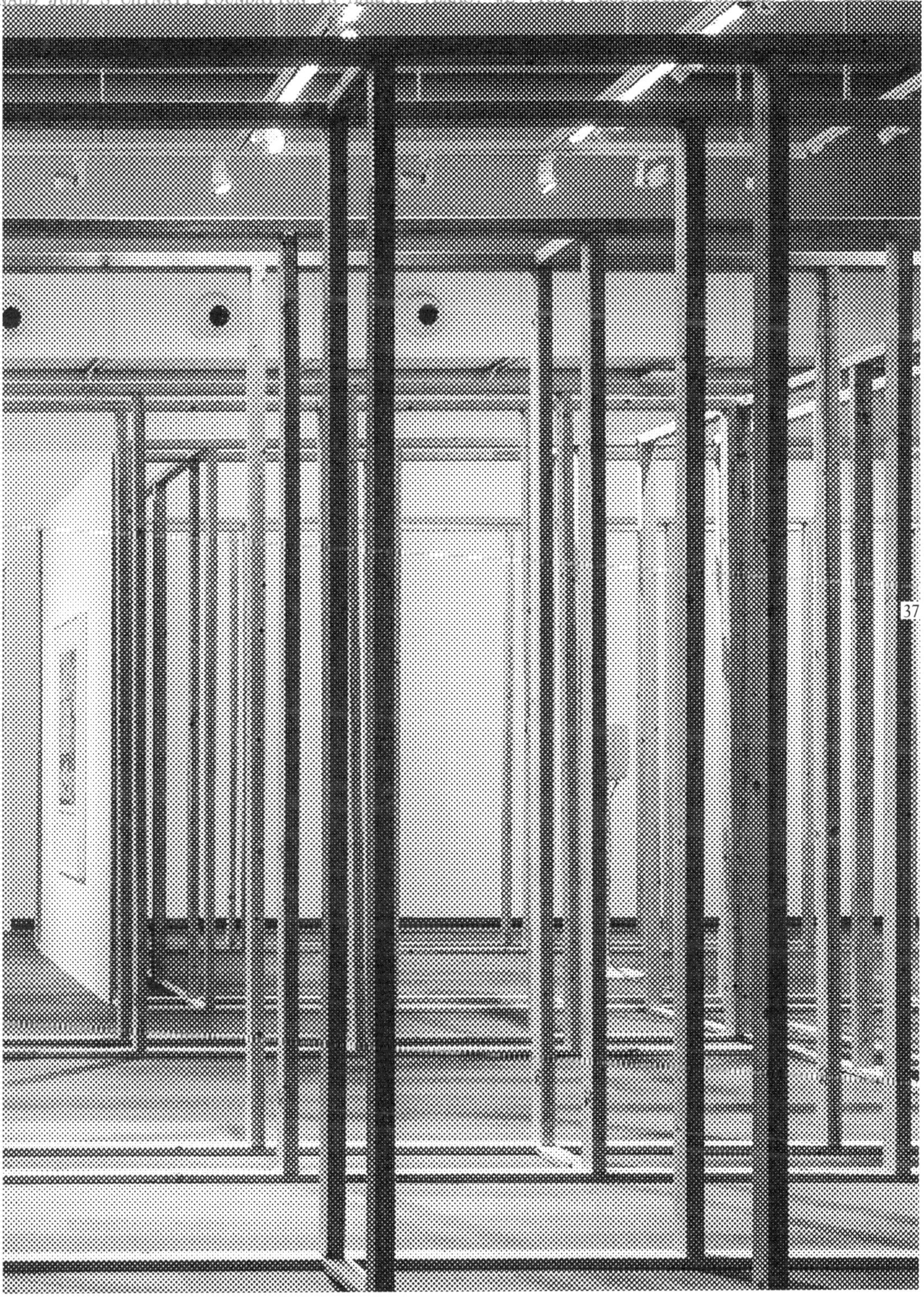

AD AND DISCUSS TEXTS BY PAUL CHAAT SMITH, LUCY LIPPARD, ROBERT IRWIN, THE SHORT STORIES OF LU

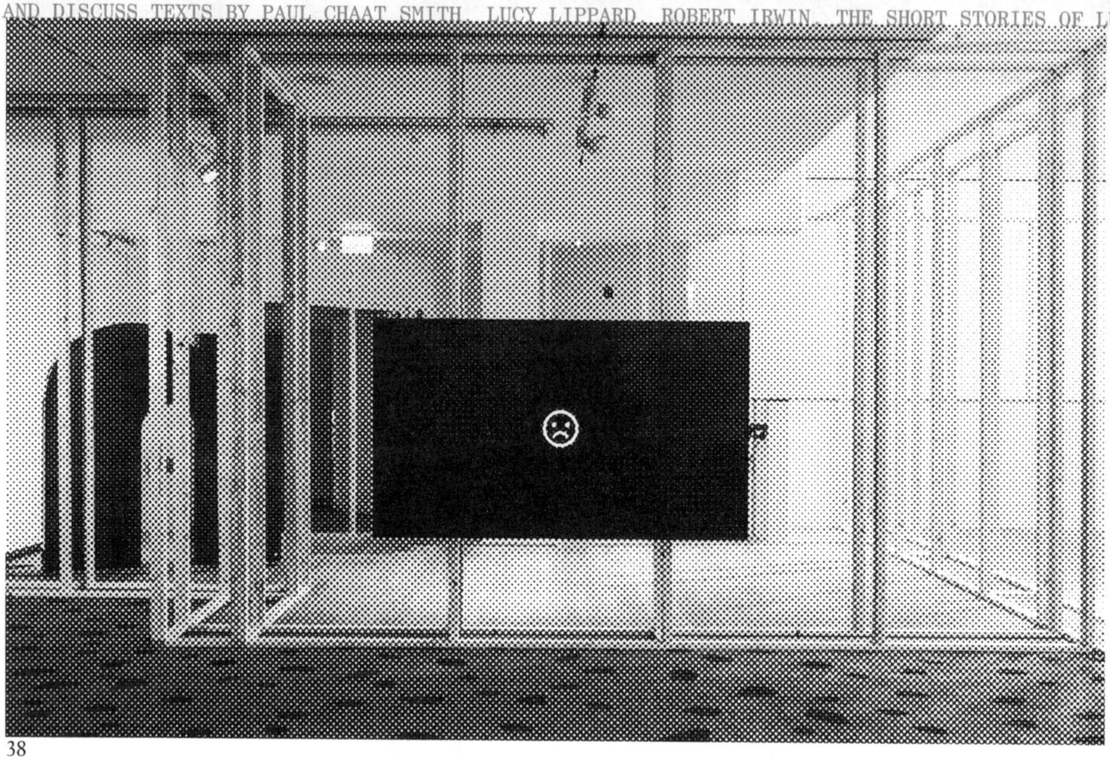

N. WHO LIVED IN BOTH ALBUQUERQUE AND EL PASO, CITIES ALSO FEATURED ON OUR BIG ADVENTURE. ANI

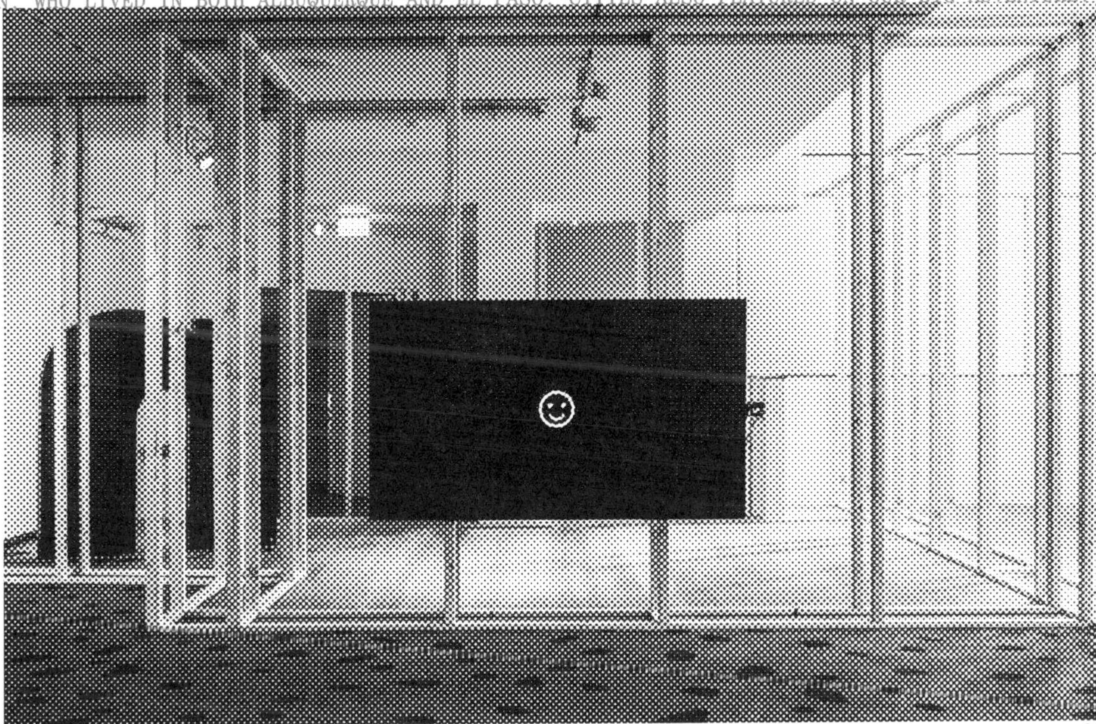

HOUGH IT'S VERY SATISFYING TO SEE STUDENTS CREATING STRONG BONDS TO ART AND ITS INQUIRIES A

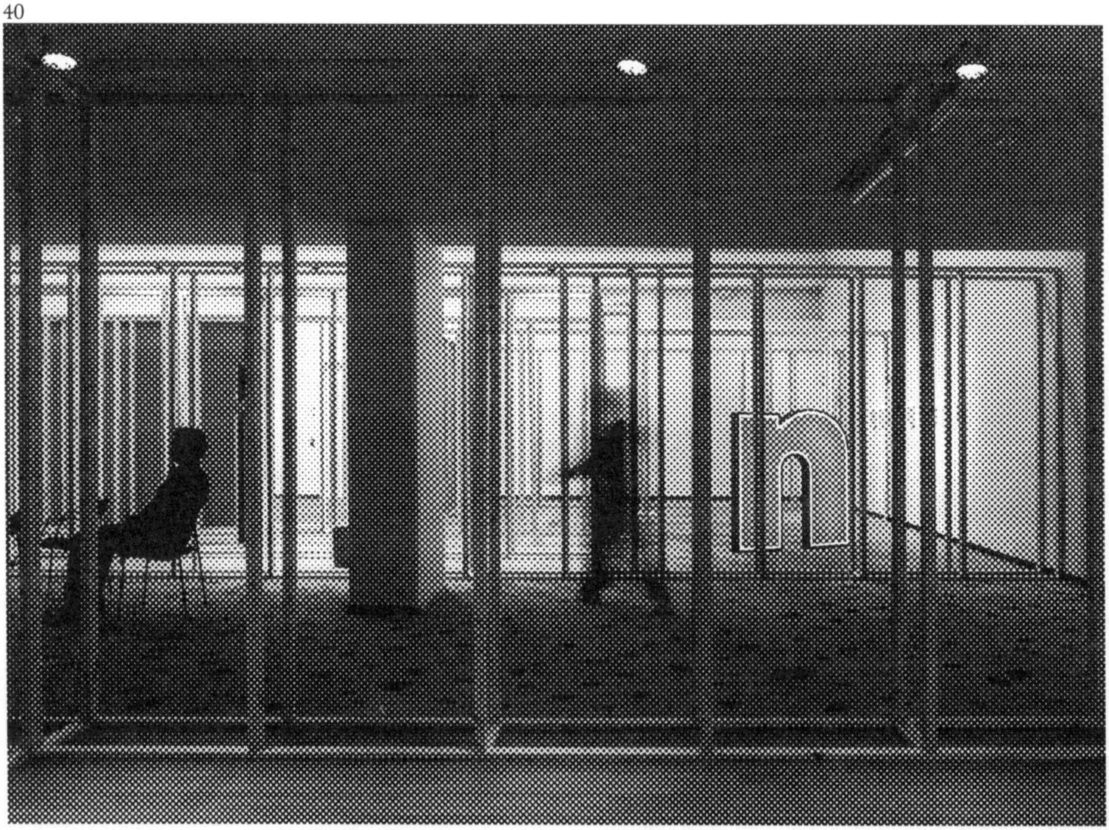

CH OTHER I'M SO LOST IN FATIGUE BY THE TIME WE PART WAYS. BUT I'M STILL DETERMINED TO FILM

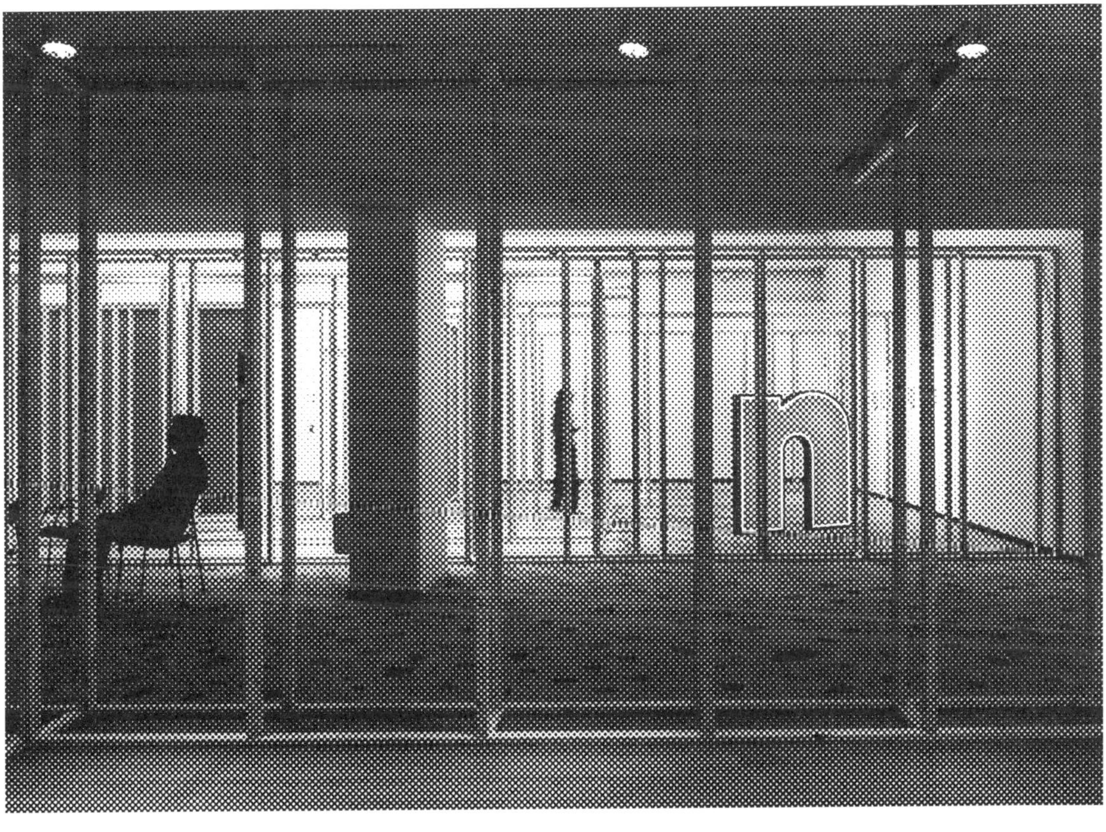

S THAT HE USED. A RATHER CLUMSY MISTAKE BUT NOT AS BAD AS PRESSING STOP INSTEAD OF RECORD.

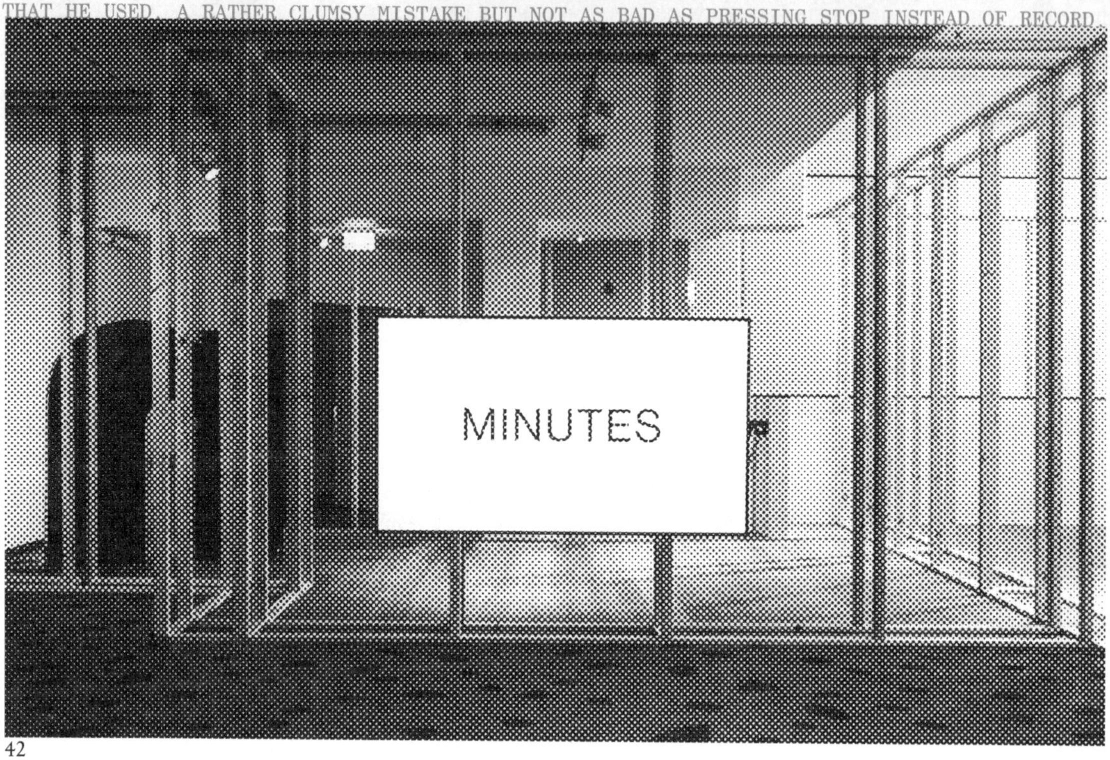

FIREWORKS] JULY FOURTH TWO-THOUSAND NINETEEN. ADRIAN AND I HEAD UP TO SAN FRANCISCO FROM

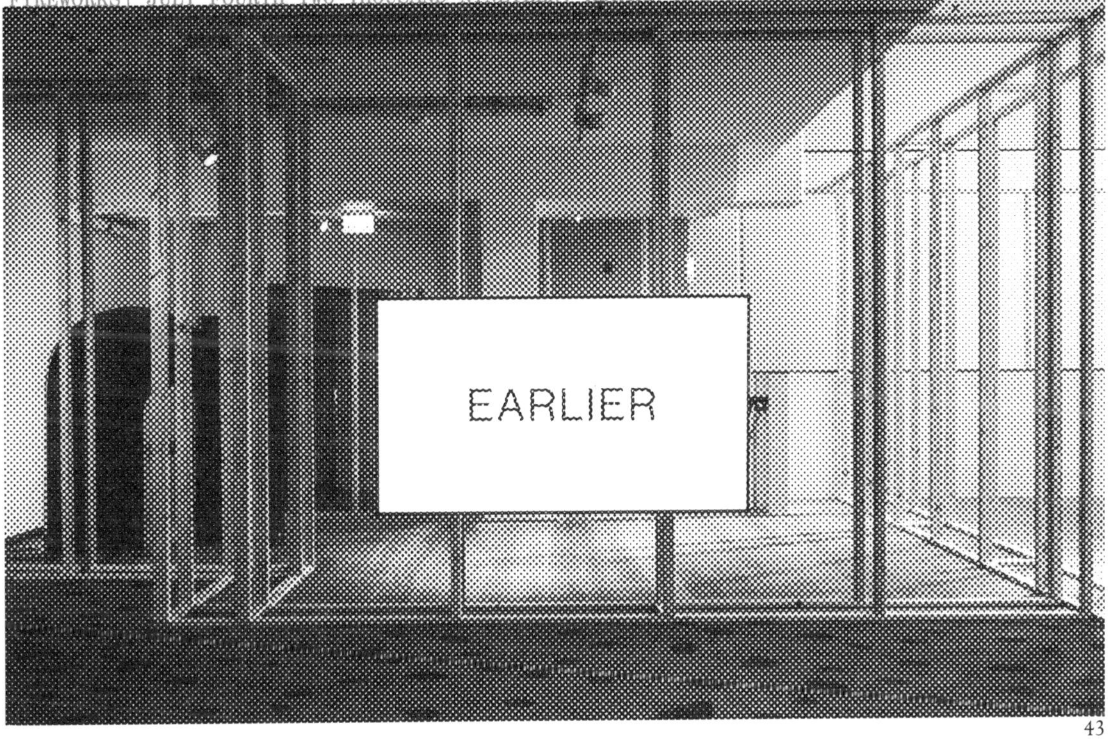

D FALLS INTO MY HANDS. ADRIAN HAS THE SHOT THOUGH. HE TEXTS ME FROM THE BACK OF THE PLANE. EX

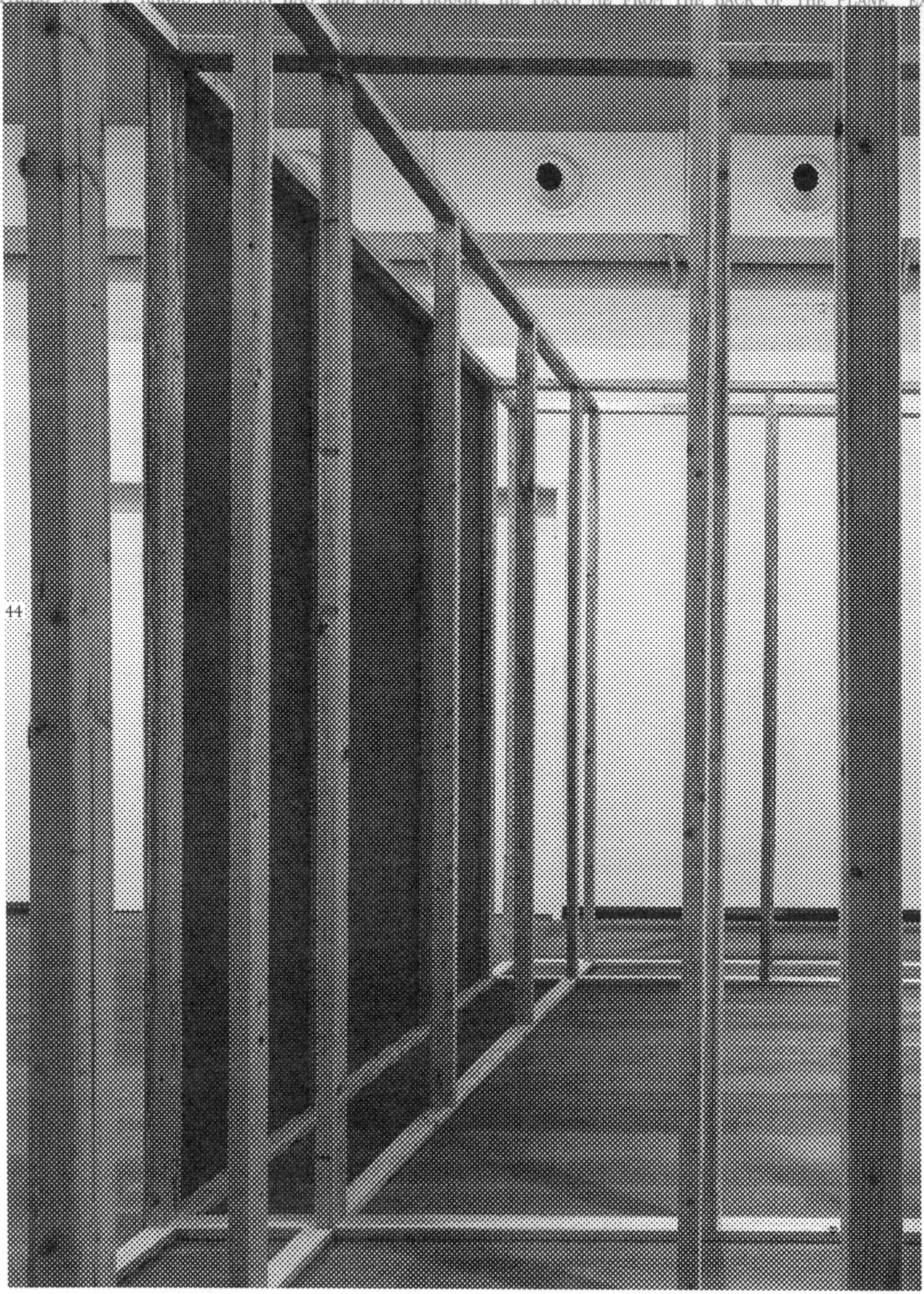

T LATER WHEN HE UPLOADS THE FOOTAGE, HE SEES HOW THE CAMERA HE RENTED WAS INCOMPATIBLE WITH T

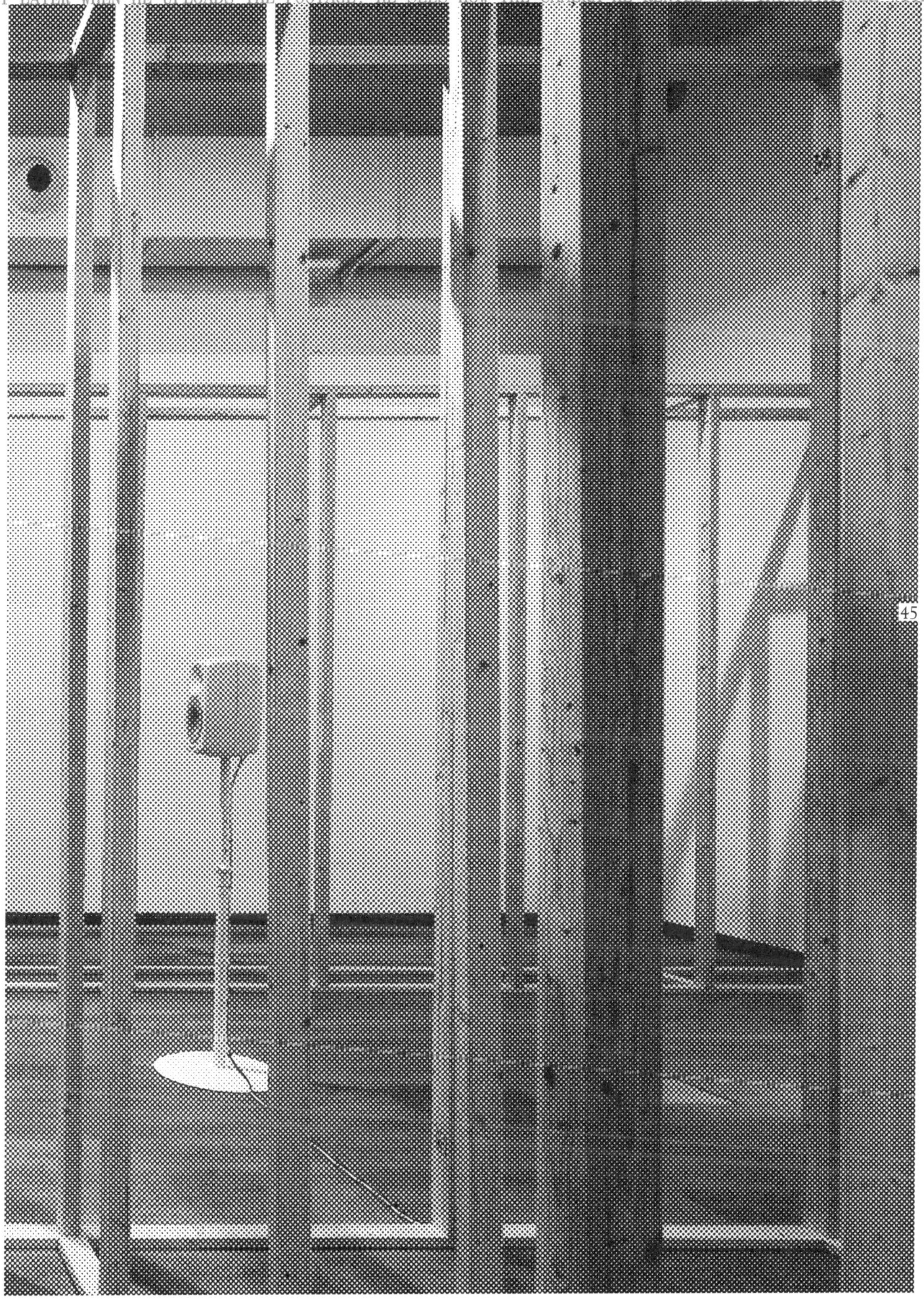

EVEN IF WE LAND UP TO TWENTY MINUTES EARLY THE SHOT WILL STILL WORK. AGAIN, I SIT IN THE FRO

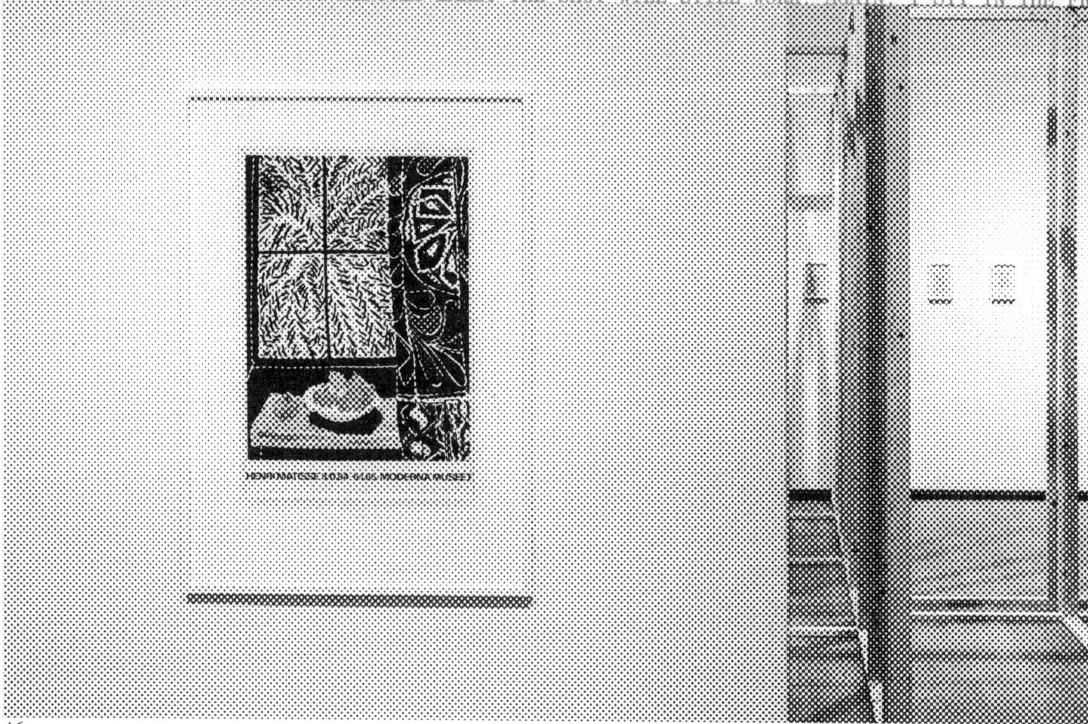

PLANE. ADRIAN IS IN THE BACK. THE PERSON SEATED NEXT TO ME TAKES A PICTURE OF A SMALL DOG

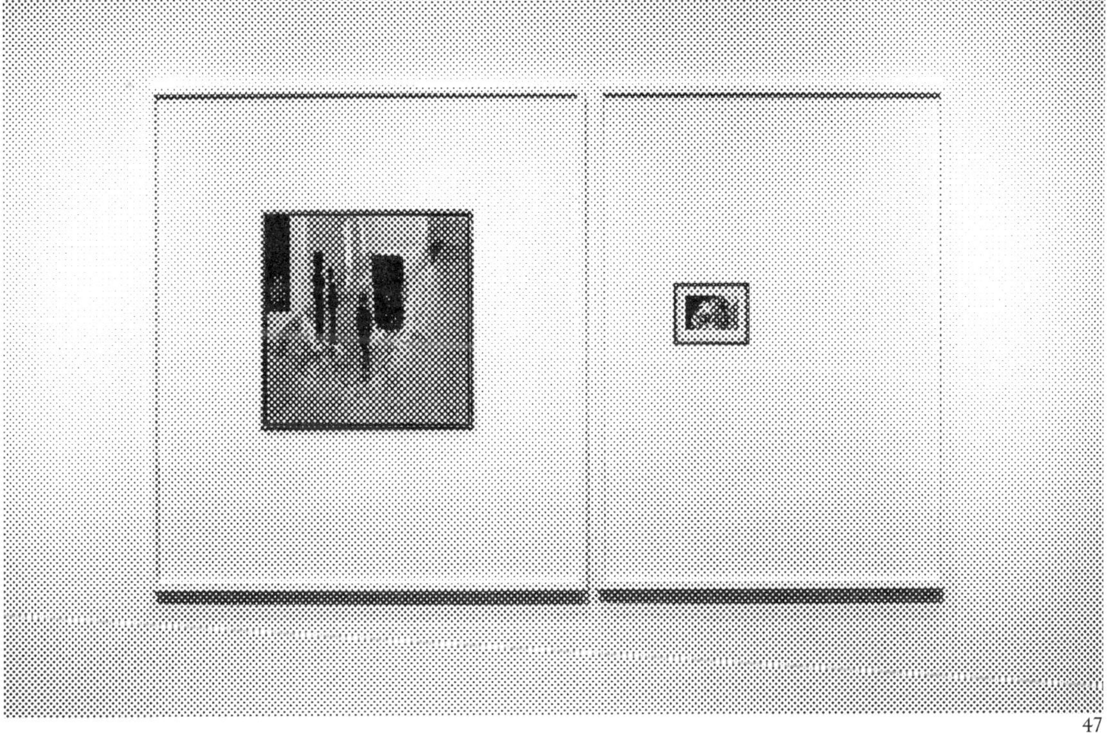

BUT IF IT'S TOO BRIGHT, THERE WON'T BE ANY FIREWORKS TO CAPTURE. I ALSO BUY A TICKET FOR MY

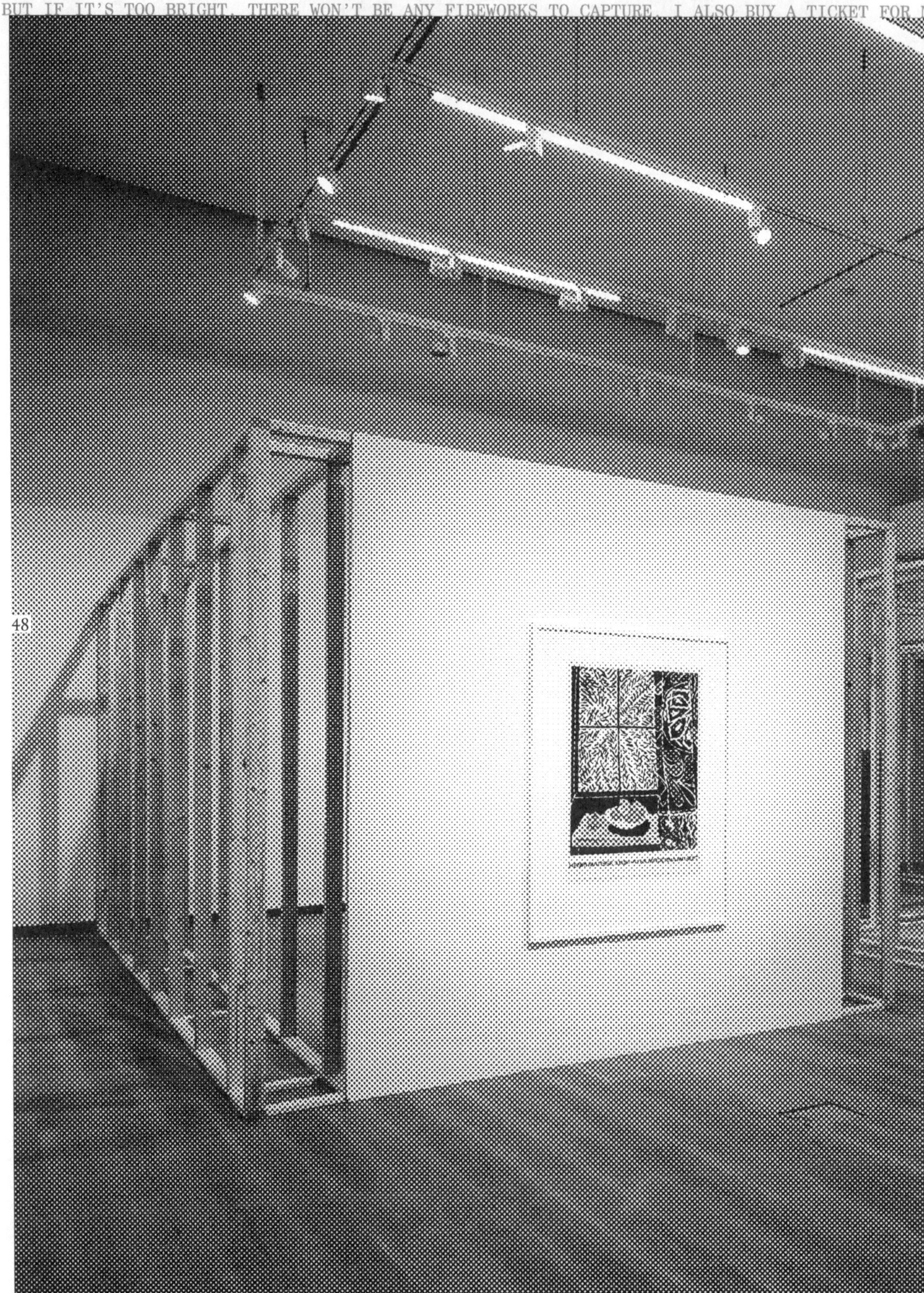

DRIAN. HE'S AGREED TO BE MY SECOND CAMERA. MY BACK UP. WE LEAVE IN THE MORNING FOR SAN FRANC

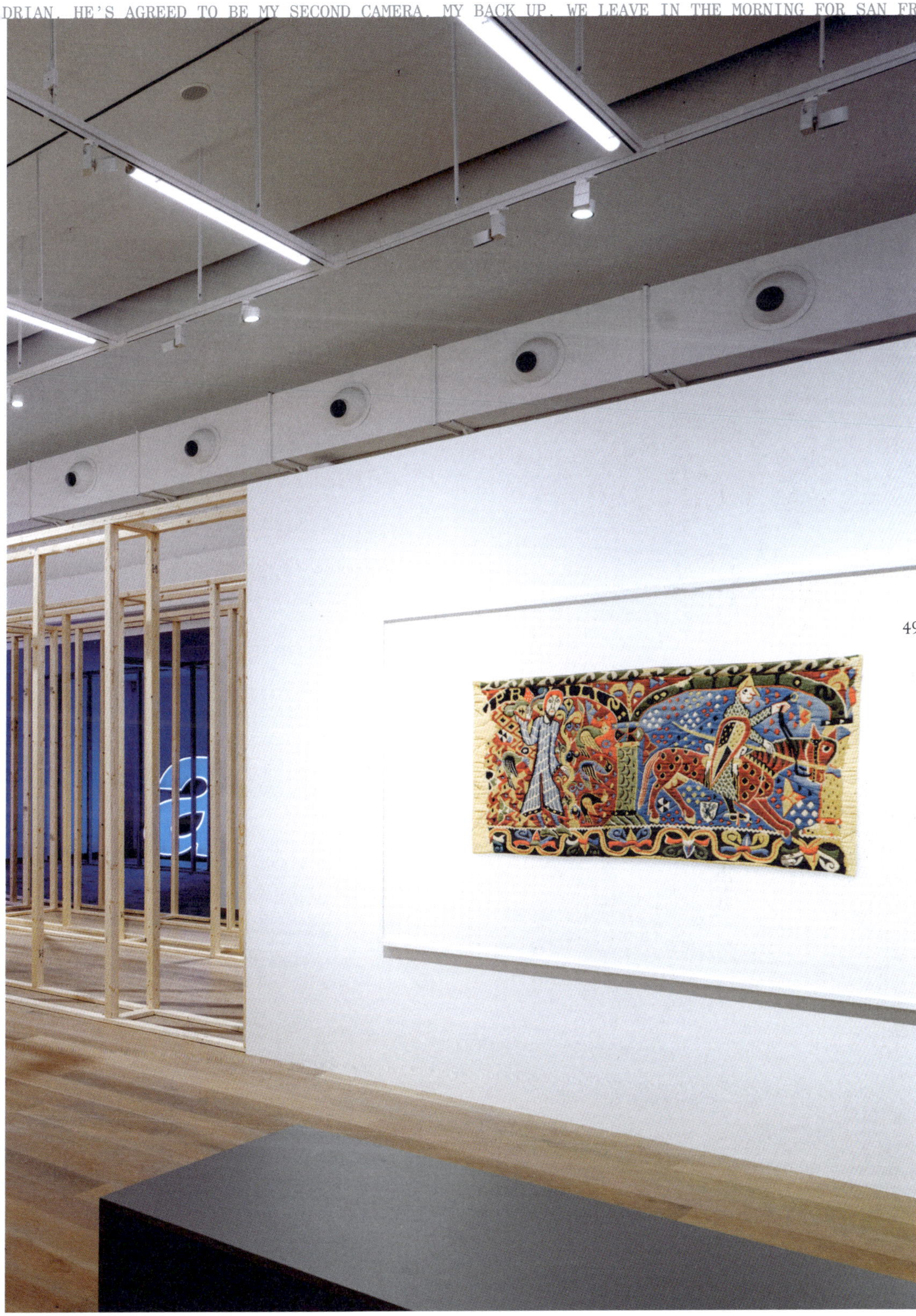

SPEND A FEW HOURS IN GOLDEN GATE PARK UNTIL IT'S TIME TO HEAD BACK TO THE AIRPORT. ON THE R

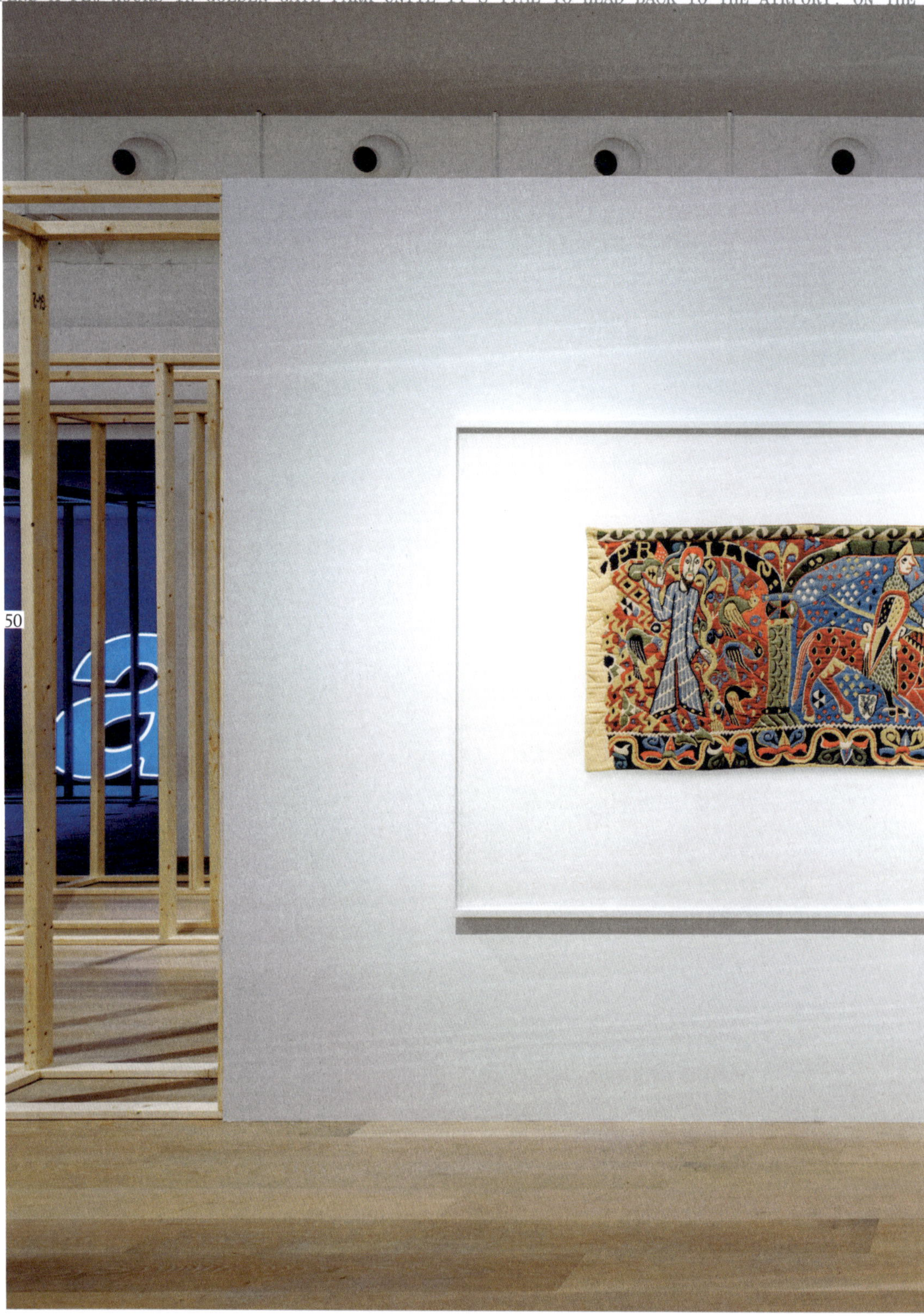

IAN SITS ON THE RIGHT SIDE OF THE PLANE IN THE BACK AWAY FROM THE WING. I SIT ON THE LEFT SI

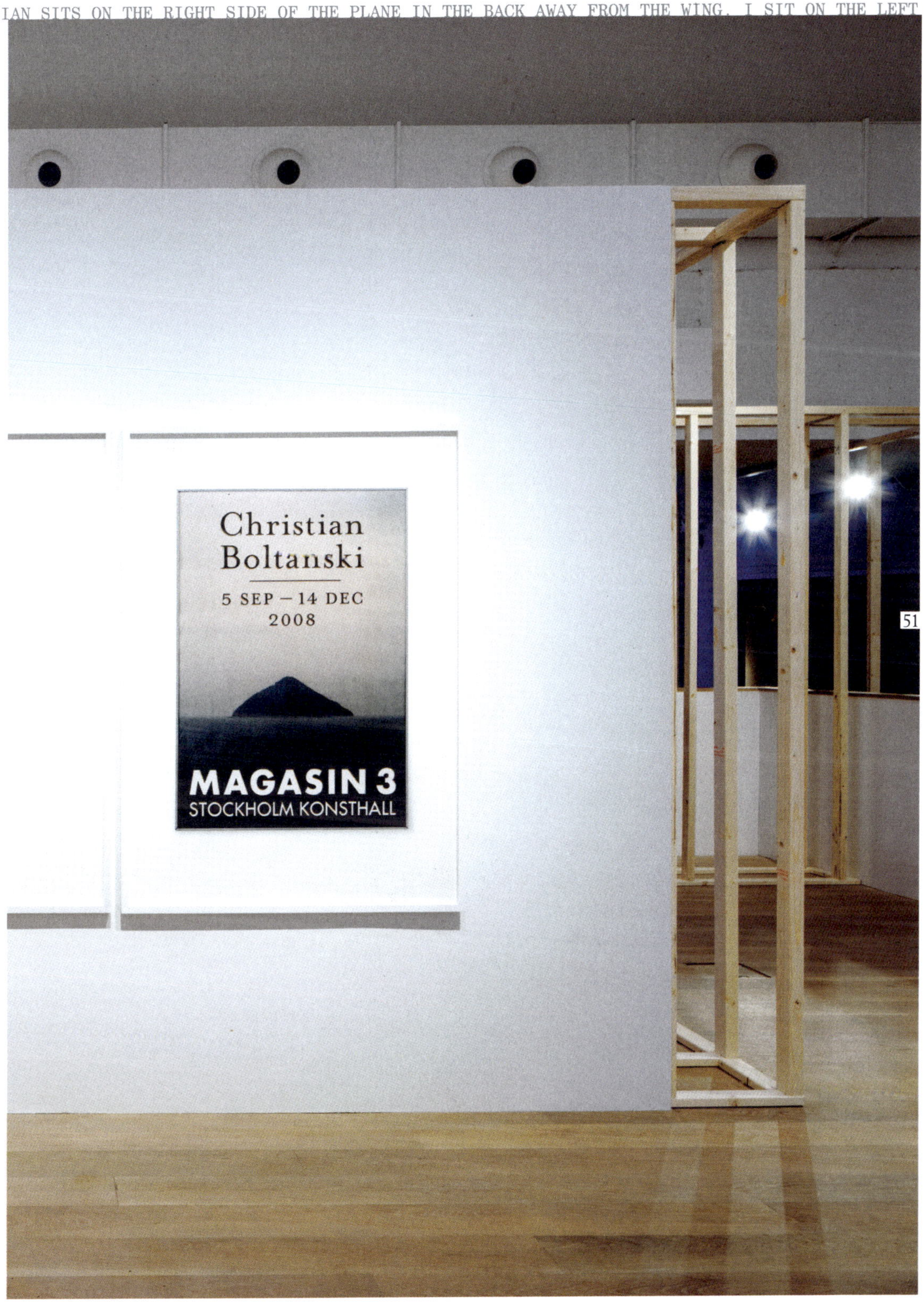

THE FRONT OF THE PLANE. A DEADHEADING PILOT TAKES THE SEAT NEXT TO ME. THE SKY IS CLEAR AS

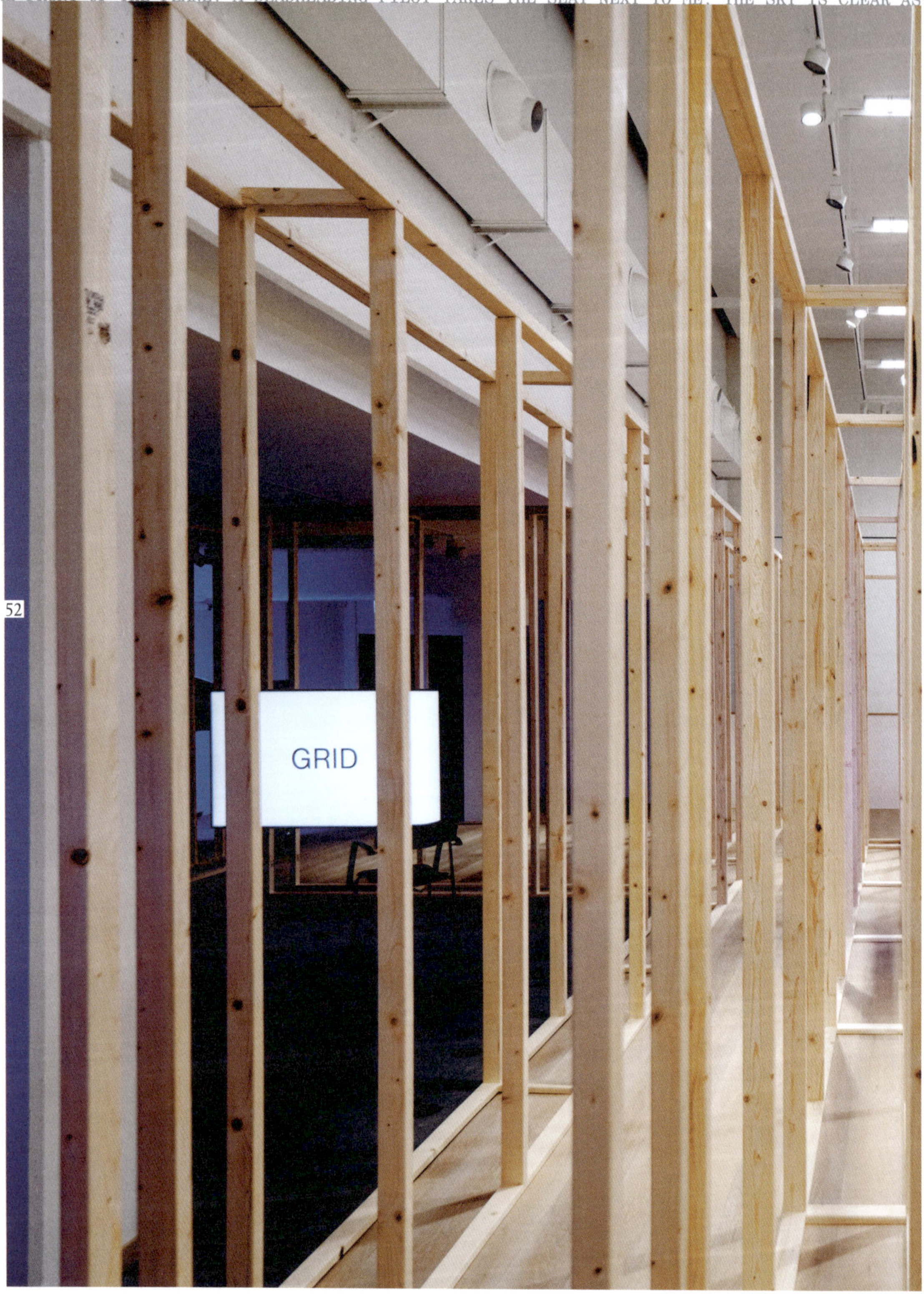

SOUTH WE FLY OVER THE CENTRAL VALLEY OF CALIFORNIA. I TEST AND ADJUST MY CAMERA. WE PASS SAN

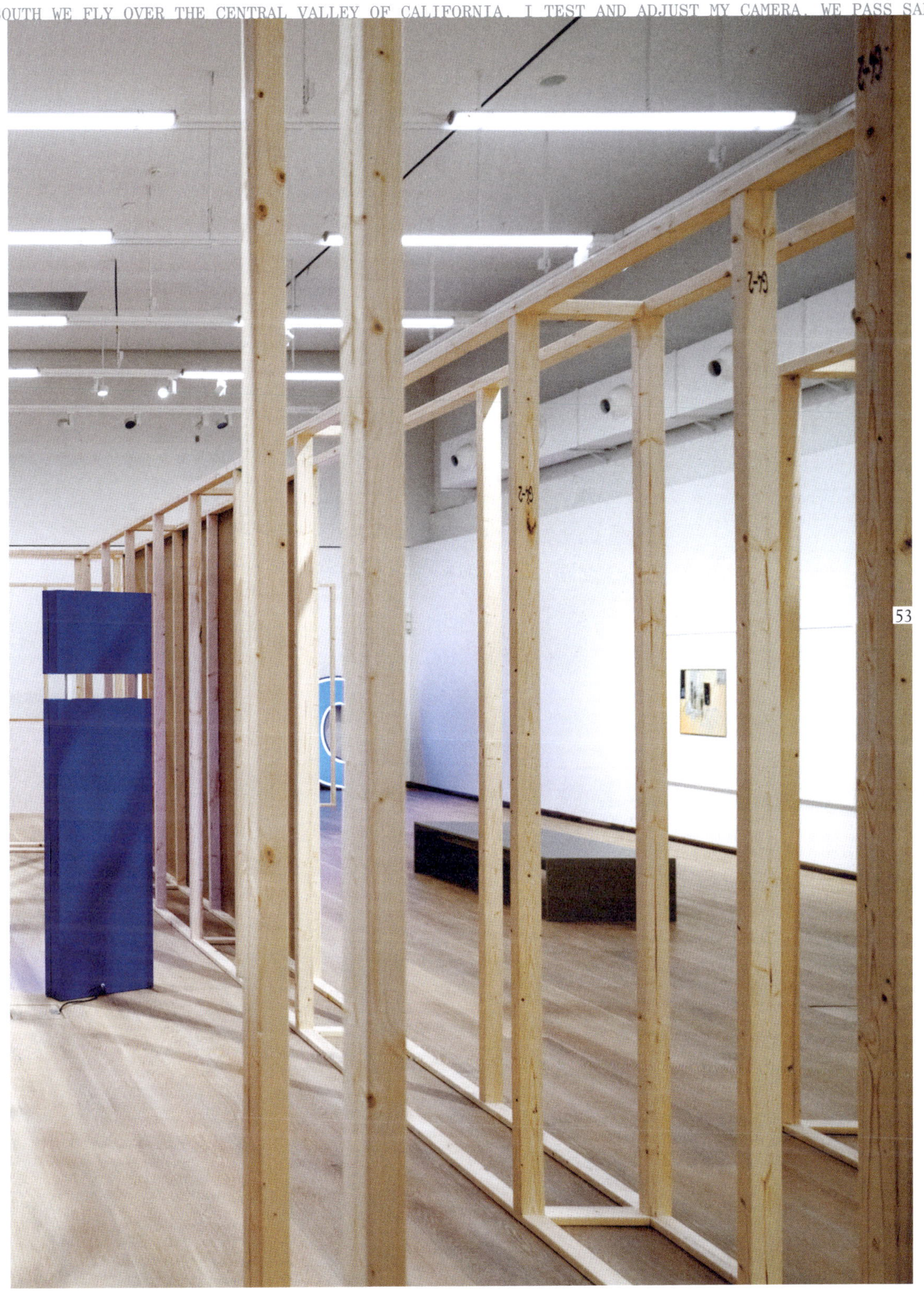

BARA, AROUND MALIBU, I FILM A SEQUENCE AND IT LOOKS GREAT. I START FILMING AGAIN DIRECTLY AFTI

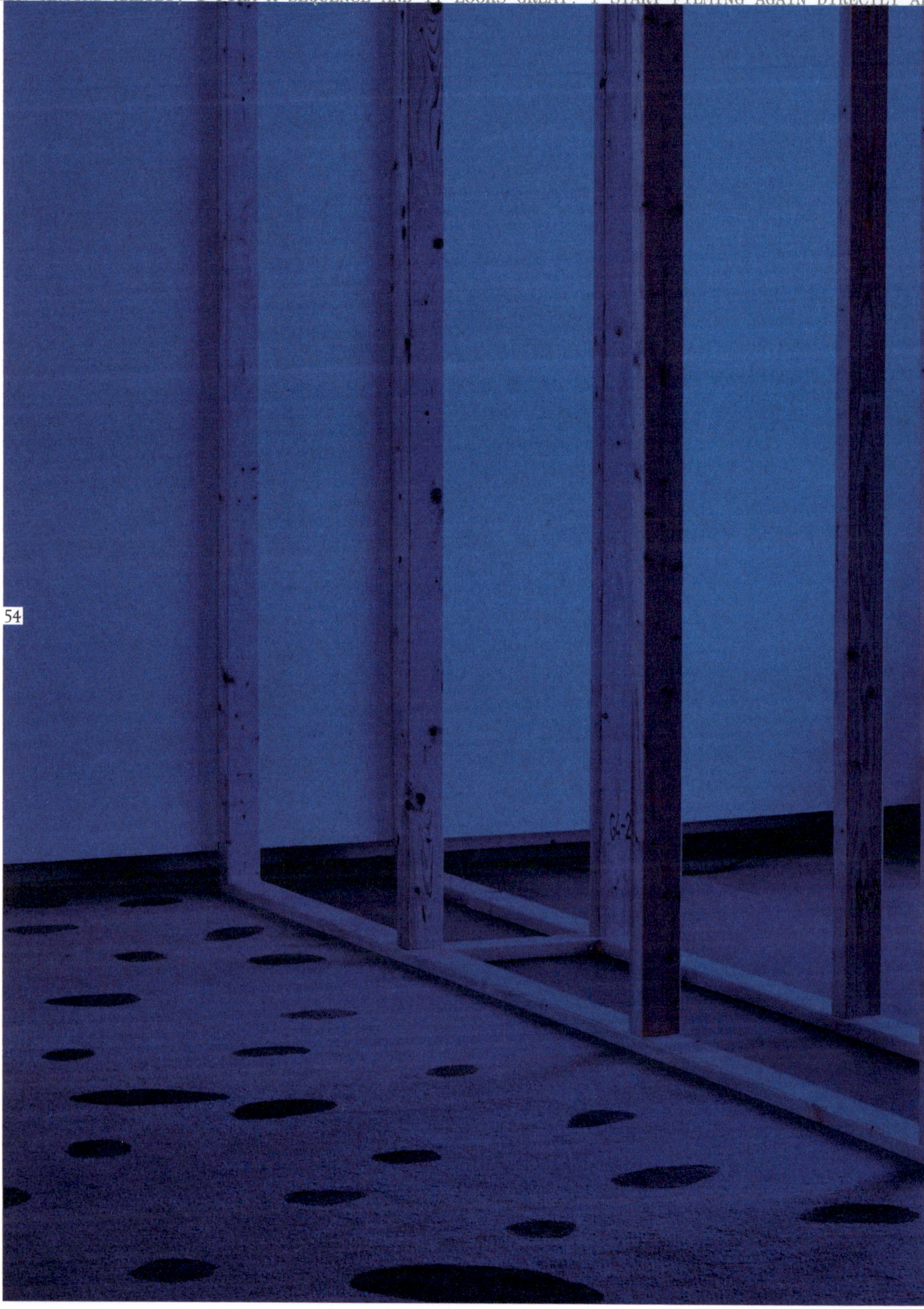

NG THE GETTY CENTER IN BRENTWOOD. THE PLANE CURVES AROUND DOWNTOWN LA TO HEAD TOWARDS THE AIRP

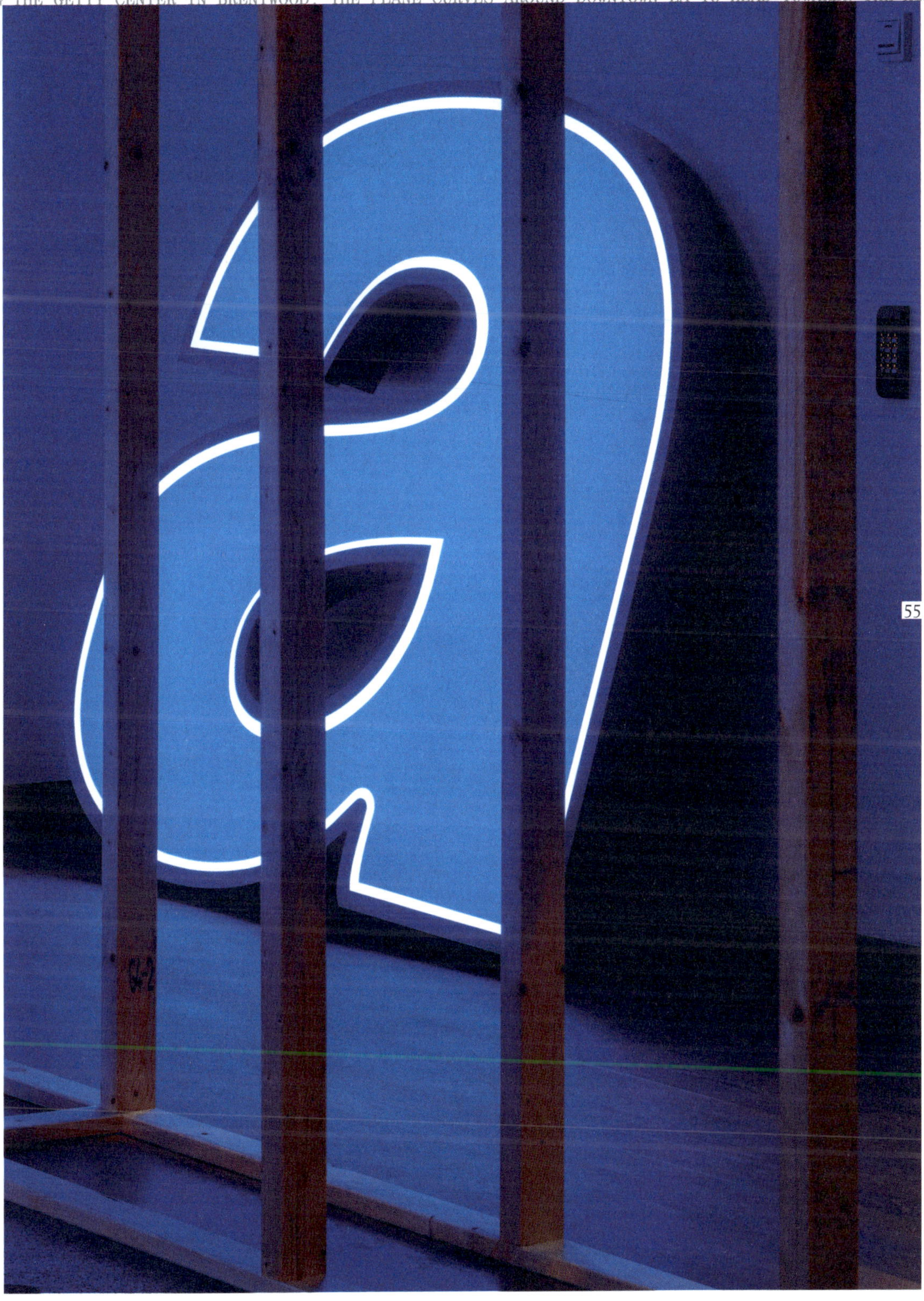

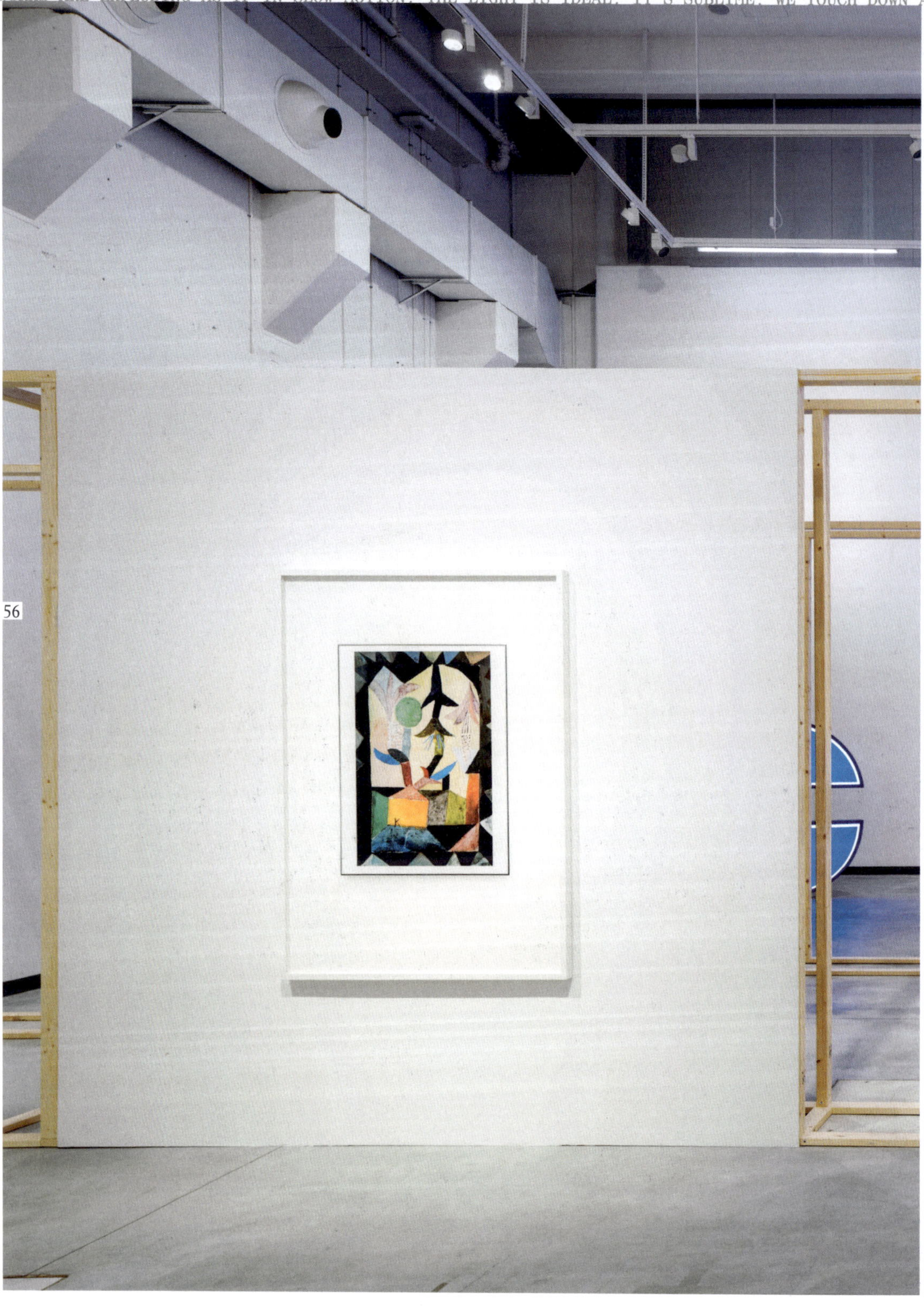

S STOP. OR I THINK I'M PRESSING STOP, BUT MY CAMERA STARTS FILMING. I'VE TOTALLY FUCKED UP. M

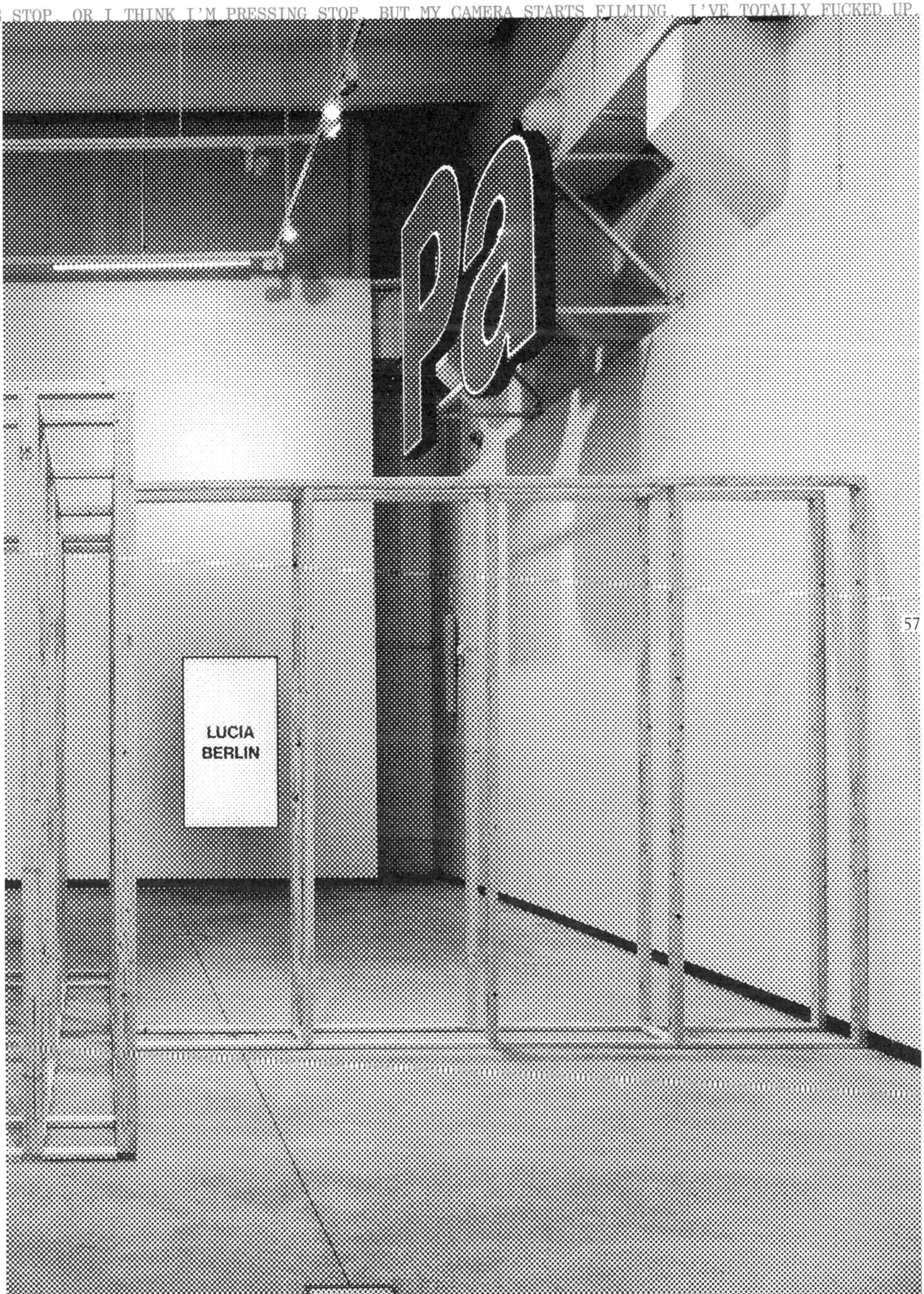

57

INDEBTED

Haytham el-Wardany

ES I LEAD A GROUP OF NINETEEN ART STUDENTS FROM SWEDEN ON AN EDUCATIONAL TRIP. WE TRAVEL FR

1.

In a room on the first floor of a building that looks out over the plateau, a man wakes up in the dark. He listens to the wind howling outside then sits up and thinks back on his dream. He was in an unfamiliar house with unfamiliar people. Tall trees lined the road as far as the eye could see. His gaze came to rest on the tree that stood directly in front of the house where he was. It was splendid and lush, its trunk slender and its branches short and densely packed. All of a sudden, the tree toppled slowly to the ground, impelled by some invisible supernatural power. He perceived each successive moment of its collapse distinctly. He heard its trunk moving through the air, he heard a thousand wings fluttering out of its path. He followed its downward trajectory with bated breath until it disappeared from sight below the windowsill. He clearly felt the sound of its branches splitting and breaking, followed by the trunk making contact with the ground, and then silence. The man in the dark room is silent. He picks up his mobile phone.

Only the people who live on the mountain know when the wind will come; they are accustomed to its yearly visit. The city-dwellers below barely notice it. Every September, the seal rattles and the wind blows in from far away. It's a delicate wind that begins to swirl and gust in the early hours, sneaking inside through windows and air vents and bringing with it a faint scent and inaudible whispers. It murmurs its way through hallways and corridors, sending eddies of sound into forgotten corners, at times like the rumble of thunder and at others like a thin, high whistle. The wind usually blows for a month of long nights, then subsides. But it is nearly spring now, and the wind shows no sign of abating. Stranger still, it seems to gather in the air shafts of residential buildings, where it roars until dawn.

—Did you notice anything carved into the trunk?
—Huh?
—The tree trunk. Was there anything written on it?
—Speak up.
—Wait, have you checked how the agribusiness sector is doing? Maybe there'll be some agribusiness firms on the "losers of the day" list.
—I already checked.
—How many people were in the house? Maybe the number means something.
—I can't remember.

Dreams are the only source of income for the people who live on the plateau. But it's no longer enough to get by on, because the wind is causing interference. Debts pile up overnight. People seem to be shrinking; their clothes hang off them. And yet they still feel more fortunate than the people in the valley below, since they don't have to work on the construction projects.

As autumn gives way to winter, the wind no longer blows only late at night but begins to whip up at sunset. In November it is a strong breeze, by December a high wind. In January it regularly blows at gale force. Its pitch is higher now, like a wail after the tears have all run dry. Windows slam open and shut.

By the time spring approaches, it has honed itself into fine blades, sharp enough to slice off a finger, which penetrate the slightest crevice in the blink of an eye. First it hisses, then it howls like a lone animal.

One day, a child stands in the queue at a supermarket, talking to the neighbors' daughter. "Do you use the app?" he asks.

"No," she replies, looking straight ahead. "But my dad does, and it's the worst. He goes on his phone the second he wakes up and sits there swiping for ages, then throws it down in a rage. Then he interrogates me about what I've dreamt to see if there are any messages."

"My mom is always complaining too," says the boy. "She's not making enough to pay off her debts anymore, because her dreams are disrupted. So now she wants me to go on the app. I don't understand how it works, though."

After the pair have paid for their shopping, they linger for a moment outside the supermarket.

"I saw a puppy yesterday," the boy says. "It was peeking out of a little red bag."

The girl smiles. "I dreamt I was counting a stack of money. It was green. I didn't recognize the currency."

They part ways, the dust hanging heavier in the air around them. The city below vibrates with the sound of diggers working on the vast new sites. Work continues twenty-four hours a day. The Administration has embarked on a huge number of excavation and construction projects; the city has never witnessed anything like it. These projects are being financed by massive loans. Streets lie open-bellied, lined with piles of earth; in the neighboring cemeteries, graves have been uncovered, the remains of their former inhabitants now pulverized and scattered to the winds. Reinforced concrete pillars, carrying new bridges and highways, tower above this chaos, and the cars that speed overhead spit out thick exhaust fumes. Polluted air rises to the plateau, and tiny particles make their way into the mountain-dwellers' nasal cavities.

Steel teeth pierce the earth's crust. Beneath lie infinite layers of debris, and through them runs a river of molten iron. Down underground, a battle is still raging. Those who have just arrived are refusing to board the ferry that will take them across the river and are now in open conflict with the Administration, which insists that departures must proceed as scheduled. The guards herd the new arrivals roughly onto the ferry, but they throw themselves into the river to get away. Since the Administration will not budge, the boats end up departing with only a few wretched passengers on board—those unable to escape—and this causes logistical problems on the other side. The newcomers are supposed to be sent immediately to their respective work sites, and if the allocation process runs behind schedule, then the work they are to perform will also run behind schedule.

Whenever the confrontation over the ferries simmers down for a while, it soon flares up again. Finally, the Administration agrees to a temporary truce. The newcomers are permitted to remain onshore until they can gather news of their comrades above ground. But the news does not reassure them.

—Very good . . . Very good . . . We're much better off these days.
—But I can't smell. My nose is blocked.
—Don't worry, it'll come back. It's a common symptom of sinusitis. The main thing is the inflammation has gone down.
—I've almost lost my voice! And I have a splitting headache.
—I can prescribe you something for the headache.
—My daughters both have the same symptoms.
—Everyone has sinusitis, I'm afraid. It's this odd weather. Just make sure to do a steam inhalation every day and gargle regularly with salt water.

I was at a noisy house party. It looked like my mother's house. Music vibrated through the walls, moving from room to room. Wherever I went, there were bodies dancing. I was looking for somewhere to sit down, and at some point I realized that there were other rooms I hadn't noticed before. I made my way into one, where I found a chimpanzee dozing peacefully. Just then, I heard shrieks outside, and I realized I needed to rouse the animal because it was the only one who could save us. Its eyes instantly flicked open and gazed up at me for a few moments. Its face was black, and its eyes bloodshot from the fug of sleep. I told it we were under attack. Suddenly alert, it leaped to its feet; it was almost my size and moved like a human. I understood then that the chimpanzee was the target of the raid.

The app's heat map function tracks fluctuations in the stock market. As values rise, they turn red and appear in relief, like elevations or mountains. Falling values are shown in blue: the deeper the blue, the lower the value. You can gauge the state of the market at a glance. The heat map settings can be changed to make it track the profit rates of a single company or subset of companies over a specific window of time, thus enabling you to identify the right investments for you. It also allows you to put together an investment portfolio according to your risk appetite and track its progress on a heat map of its own.

—Didn't it say anything?
—Didn't what say anything?
—The chimpanzee.
—No.
—A lot of brands have animals in their name or logo.
—That's the problem. I don't know which company it's about.
—Dreams have got harder. The quality's not what it was.
—Huh?
—Dreams. Poor quality.
—The lady on the fourth floor's moving out. I saw her today with all her stuff.

The underground truce doesn't last long. The Administration resumes transports across the river, while the newcomers have lain down on the riverbank, still refusing to board the ferry. They know from those who have gone before that if they cross the river, they will be forced to write dreams forever. The Administration threatens to use force against the strikers. Suddenly, in the subterranean darkness, the strikers hear the sound of digging up above. They stand up, and begin to move toward the source of the sound. They walk for a long time; the path grows narrower and the roof lower, until they are crawling through caves and tunnels in the rock. They don't look back. Finally, they see the colossal Rock of Arrival above their heads. This is as far as they can go. They stand at the opening between the worlds, which is sealed tightly shut by the Rock. On the surface, steel teeth whirr and grind, while bodies crawl below, and between the two worlds is a seal neither can transgress. The strikers are silent, unsure of what to do.

Just then, a group of pebbles who have joined the crawling strikers have an idea. They bounce into the air and knock against certain parts of the Rock, then wait for a response. There is a long silence before it deigns to speak. In the language of rocks, it tells them it shifts ever so slightly for one month each year to honor an agreement made with the generations who crawled there before them. When the strikers hear this, they settle in their places. And indeed, when autumn comes around, the Rock of Arrival turns and shifts a few millimeters. Three pebbles roll themselves into the crack to stop the seal closing tight again. Then the strikers crawl all the way back.

By the following autumn, most of the residents of the building that looks out over the plateau have left. They've moved to the valley below, looking for work on one of the construction sites. Ever since their dreams began to go awry and the app stopped bringing in money, they haven't been able to afford the rent. The wind is practically a hurricane now, and the city-dwellers too can hear its constant roar. The few who remain in their apartments have tried to stop up all the gaps so it can't get in.

One morning, the man who lives on the first floor wakes after a night of fitful sleep and looks out over a city now almost entirely submerged in dust. He is regarding this vast brown cloud with bloodshot eyes when he notices balloons rising from the valley—giant, heavyweight helium balloons, like you see at car dealerships and store openings. He can make out writing; at first he can't read what it says, but the balloons are rising, and soon they are level with his window. The writing says: PAY IT ALL BACK.

J'RE NOT FAMILIAR WITH WHAT A CUDDLE THERAPIST IS, IT'S A PERSON WHO SOMEONE HIRES TO HOLD THEM

2.

Thank you for your letter, and apologies for taking so long to write back. Thank you, too, for your perceptive observations on what I am calling *the language of the dead.* Today I'd like to tell you about something that happened to me recently, which left quite a mark, and which I think gets to the heart of our subject.

I am preoccupied by a scene from the *Narrative of the Life of Frederick Douglass* in which he recounts how he and his fellows would walk to Great House Farm to receive their monthly allowances. On the way, they would fill the woods with their singing, thereby breaking the ban on music imposed by the whites, who had always sensed danger when they heard the beat of the enslaved people's drums. As they walked, they would improvise heart-rending laments that wove together fragments of half-remembered melodies and lyrics. "They would sometimes sing the most pathetic sentiment in the most rapturous tone, and the most rapturous sentiment in the most pathetic tone," writes Douglass.[1] 1

Frederick Douglass, *Narrative of the Life of Frederick Douglass, an American Slave*, in *The Classic Slave Narratives*, ed. Henry Louis Gates Jr. (New York: Mentor Books, 1987), 262–63.

In this scene, Douglass's fellows must have been drawing from the repertoire of "sorrow songs," described by W.E.B. Du Bois as "veiled and half articulate" expressions of an "unvoiced longing," which were sung by African Americans during the centuries of enslavement.[2] Over the decades, the words and melo-

W.E.B. Dubois, *The Souls Of Black Folk* (Oxford University Press, 2007), 171, 169. 2

dies of these songs often came loose and switched places; their lyrics sometimes 63
contained incomprehensible phrases that may have originated in beliefs from the past. Yet these songs had an uncanny power to transmit coded messages of hope to those living in misery and captivity.

It is precisely this aspect of that moving scene from Douglass's life which holds my attention: the songs' uncanny ability to pluck at the past as it rises to the surface of the present, as if some power rests in the flotsam of forgotten words and the jetsam of long-lost melodies out of which they are constructed, allowing them to speak so clearly to the present that they can fill the hearts of those who hear them with "ineffable sadness."[3] This feeble power, passed down

Douglass, *Narrative of the Life of Frederick Douglass*, 262–63. 3

through the generations, is another language of the dead we must learn.

I'm telling you all this so as to explain how I felt when I recently heard an interview with the poet Fu'ad Haddad, sent to me by my friend the Crow. As I listened, it occurred to me that breath, like song, might also be a place where that strange power could make itself felt.

I don't know the exact date of the interview, but I'm guessing it was late in the poet's life—Haddad died in 1985. As I listened, I suddenly found my attention wandering to the sound of his breath in the gaps between words. His inhalations sounded like he had come up against a solid obstacle. He breathed as though he was calling to the outside world for help. Each inhalation was a gasp, an incomprehensible cry for assistance that bubbled up from the deep. Every breath said *we are in trouble, and we can't get out of it alone.* Despite the solid obstacle, his lungs finally seemed to fill with air, and his thoughts on poetry and language would come tumbling out. Exhalations are a vehicle for speech; inhalations are a vehicle for the appeals for help that are the foundation of speech. When talking about his work, Haddad speaks clearly, but something obscure lingers at the end of each exhalation, each idea. Something hovers at the end of his sentences. Something which made him realize, perhaps, that the trouble we're in is too big to be breathed away. And then the respiratory cycle begins again.

Why did I suddenly become aware of the poet's breathing? It's noticeable that so many of the epidemics of the twenty-first century—swine flu, bird flu, MERS, and Covid-19—have been respiratory conditions. Airborne diseases are nothing new, but they seem to be appearing in novel forms ever more rapidly. I wonder what it is that makes breath the site where the failure of life on earth as a shared endeavor should choose to express itself? So many creatures, human and otherwise, are exhausted and breathless. Harsh conditions have turned their bodies into incubators for new diseases that quickly spread. Meanwhile, other creatures—mainly humans—live in prosperity and comfort.

Haddad's rasping breath is charred by tobacco and the vicissitudes of the times he lived through. He wrote about the poor and the oppressed and was repeatedly imprisoned in the 1950s and 1960s for communist activity. The air he inhales has been breathed by others before him—some still alive, some long dead. You can feel the fire blazing within it. What gives such expressive force to a barely audible breath like this? Where does its fire come from? Why is it at certain moments so distinctly audible, while speech retreats into the background?

Why is it that breath can go where words cannot?

In the interview, as Haddad discusses the relationship between the vernacular Egyptian Arabic in which he writes and standard Arabic, his words are punctuated by short breaths no less eloquent than either, and I think of Du Bois's "unvoiced longing." Unvoiced it may be, but this longing resides in any language that wants to unsettle the status quo. As I listen to Haddad speaking and breathing, it becomes clear to me that language is not just words. Something else is carried alongside or within words—something that cannot be heard, or perhaps is not allowed to be. Something like the murmurs of comrades lost to silent deaths after the Egyptian regime stripped them of their voices. Or the rumblings of those who died long before, those who tried and failed, those excised from history by the victors. Like the incomprehensible lyrics of the sorrow songs—"slight words or mere doggerel," Du Bois calls them—his breaths are charged with the force of endeavors past, of lives that resisted injustice until they broke.[4] Haddad restores lost vowels—sighs, moans, murmurs, and screams—

4 Dubois, *The Souls Of Black Folk*, 171.

to the Arabic language. He learned them from those around him, as well as those further afield. He wrote in solidarity with liberation movements in Palestine, Vietnam, and Africa and supported Mohammad Mosaddegh's nationalization of the Iranian oil industry. Till his very last breath, Haddad strove to bring his individual voice together with the voices of all these people.

The interview has helped me make sense of a dream I once had about Haddad. I don't think I've ever told you about it. Not much happened in the dream, or at least not much I can recall. All I remember is his thick glasses and what he said to me: *The world is like it is because one of us borrowed fifty piastres from an animal and still hasn't paid it back.* Perhaps this longstanding debt is an allegory for our responsibility toward those no longer with us. To repay the debt would be to acknowledge the consequences of an entire history of hegemony, violence and injustice. It's the only debt worth repaying. Like the feeble power that is passed from one generation to the next, from one species to another, the debt is passed on.

Those with an ear for the blossoming and breaking of longing can detect something other than ill health in Haddad's breathing. I'm not the only one. Our ears have been honed by experiences of collective endeavor and failure, of hope and defeat. They can hear what has been silenced and forgotten. In a world abandoned by poetry, these ears can perceive it where it is least expected, even in the cracks of a person's labored breathing. In these hidden clefts, poetry is at work, laboring hard to pass on that feeble power. Isn't this what it must mean to learn the language of the dead?

In the poem "Ayn Shams" from *Days of Wonder and Death*, Haddad says: "My eyelids are neither asleep nor awake / In the lake are my crocodile's tears / My song is the shape of what I've lost." Do sorrow songs not also seek a shape for what is lost? Or, better, are they not a taking-shape of loss itself? What did Haddad lose? Poetry? Fellow travelers? The road itself? The past? Revolution? Justice? Happiness? Perhaps all these things. But this poem, or indeed this whole book of poetry, is not an elegy or a lament. Rather, like a sorrow song, it transform the defeats and losses of the past into energy, offering hope to those who know how to listen.

The interview with Fu'ad Haddad, and his breathing, is still playing in my mind, and I will write more to you about it. It has also prompted me to write a new story for the collection I'm working on, though I'm still unsure about it. I enclose a draft of the story with this letter. I hope to hear what you think of it soon.

Yours,
M

HER EVERY QUESTION I CAN THINK OF. HOW DID YOU GET INTO THIS LINE OF WORK? HOW LONG IS EACH S

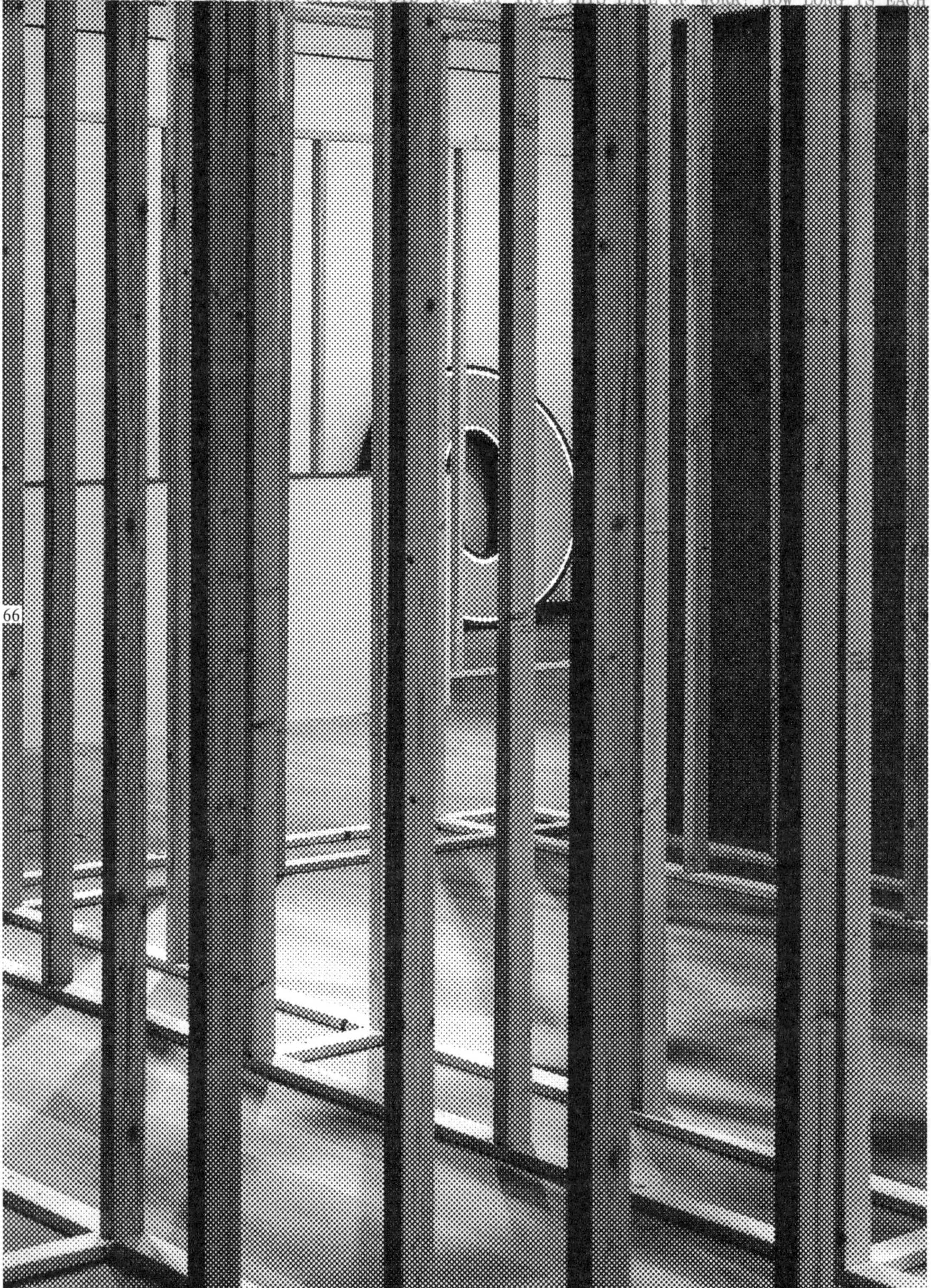

HOW OLD ARE YOUR CLIENTS? HOW DO YOU GET YOUR CLIENTS? HER ANSWER TO THIS LAST QUESTION MAKES

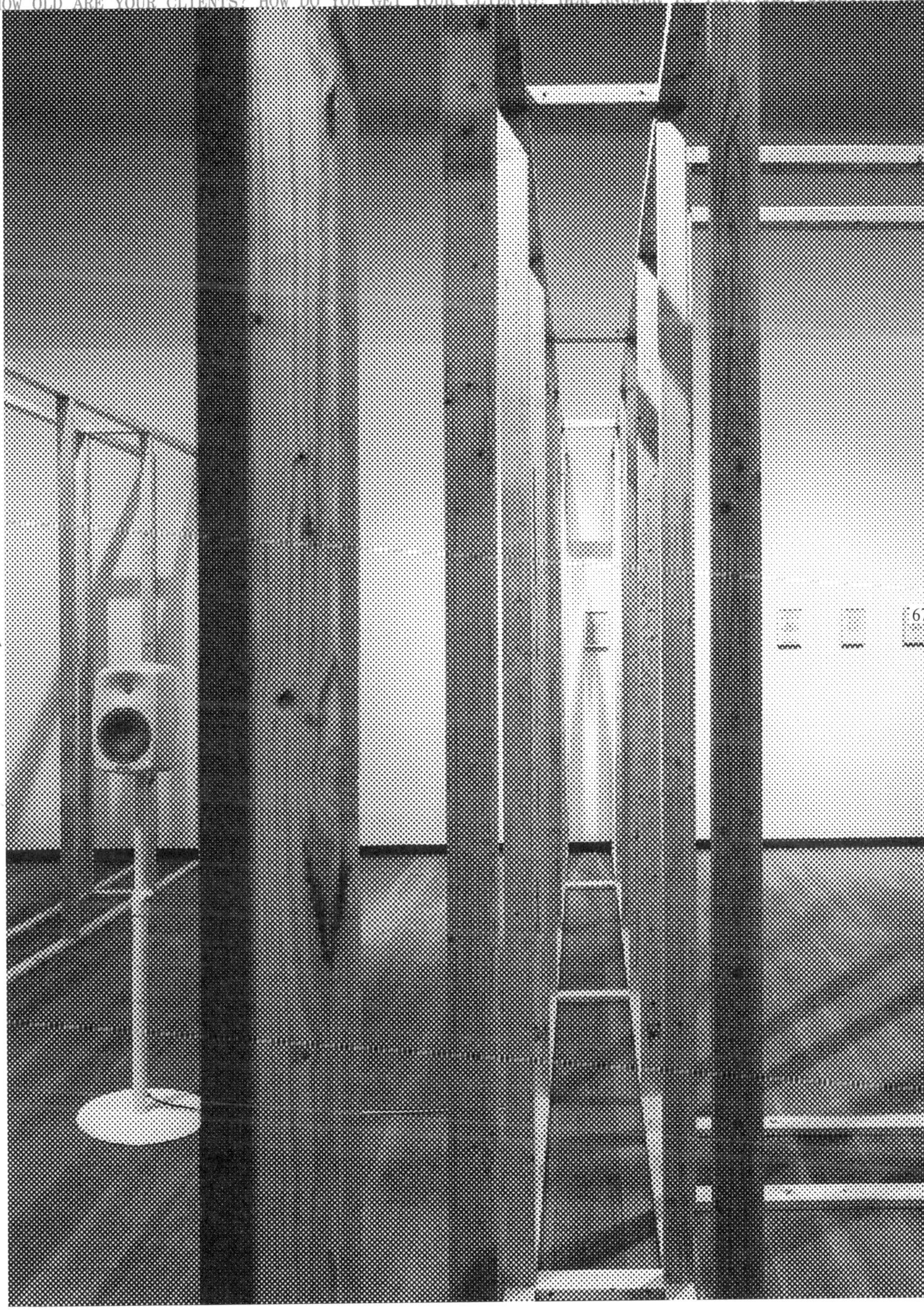

E IN FRONT OF US. IT'S OBVIOUSLY AN EMOTIONAL SUPPORT ANIMAL. WE START TALKING ABOUT THE CU

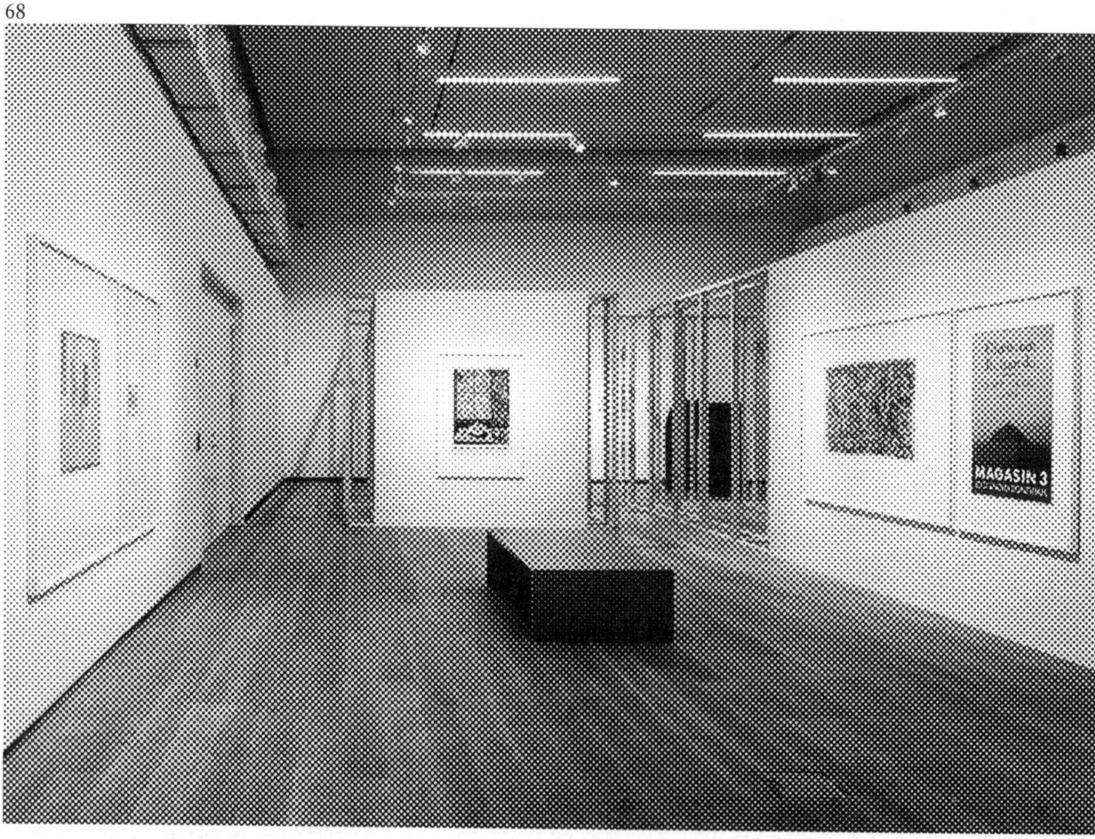

HE'S CHATTY IN THAT AMERICAN WAY THAT I REALLY MISS THESE DAYS. SHE OPENLY TELLS ME WHAT SHE D

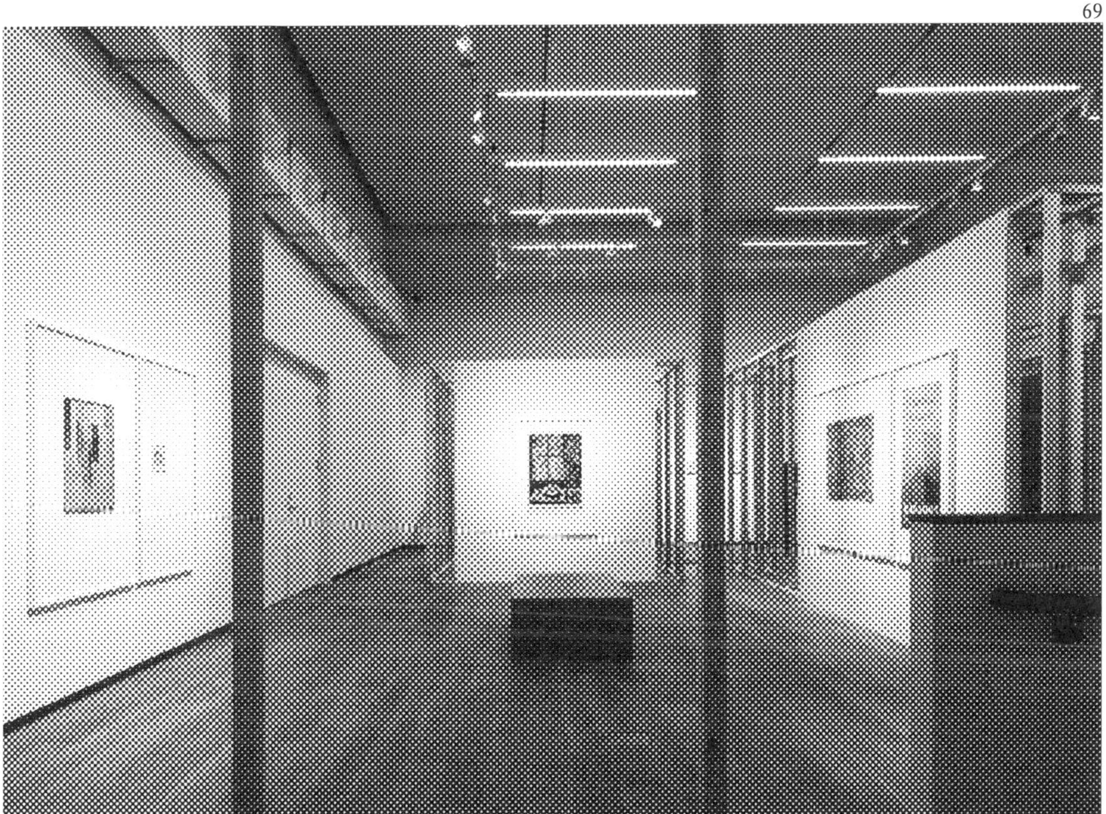

TOCKHOLM, WHICH IS WHERE WE ALL LIVE TO ALBUQUERQUE, NEW MEXICO OUR FIRST POINT OF ENTRY. F

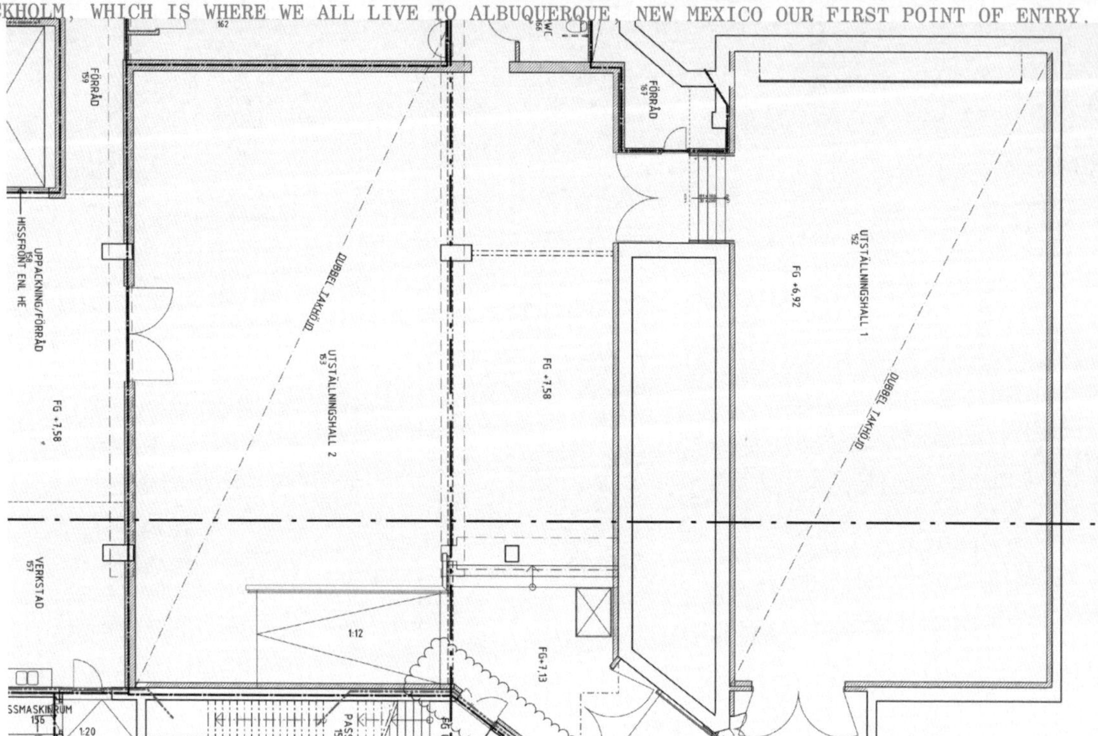

E WE DRIVE NORTH TO SANTA FE. AND THEN EVEN FURTHER NORTH TO A REMOTE VILLAGE CALLED ABIQU

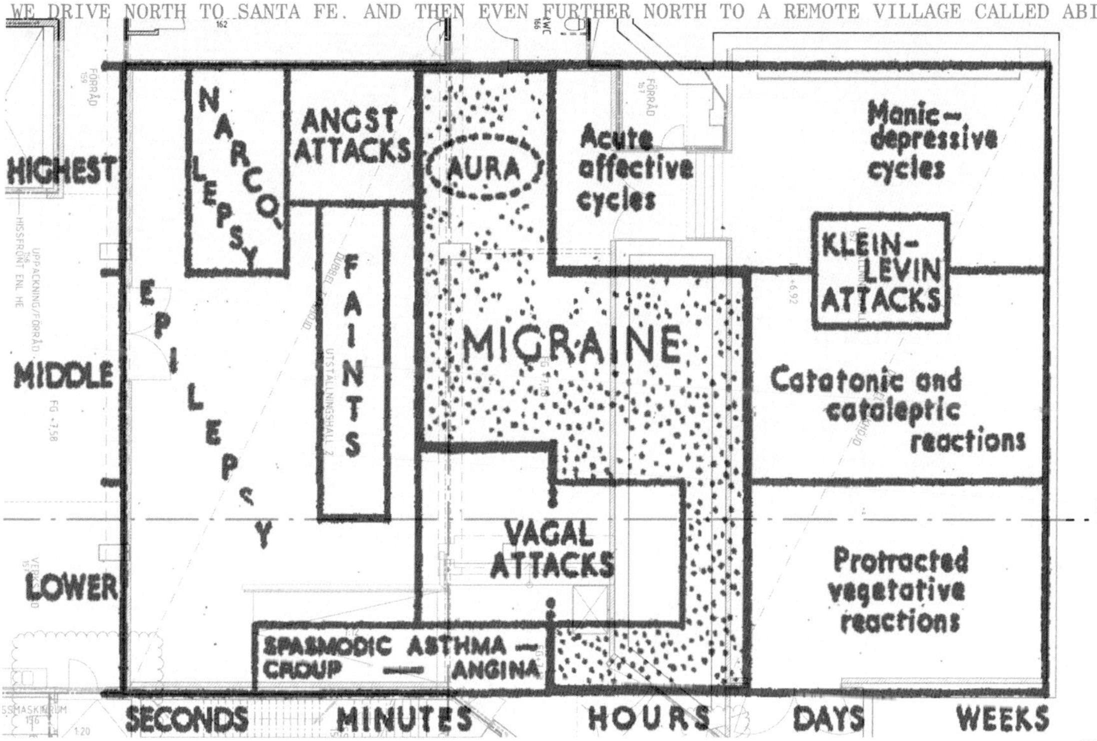

SHE TELLS ME THAT HER CLIENTS FIND HER BY WORD-OF-MOUTH. I TRY TO IMAGINE THE CIRCUMSTANCE

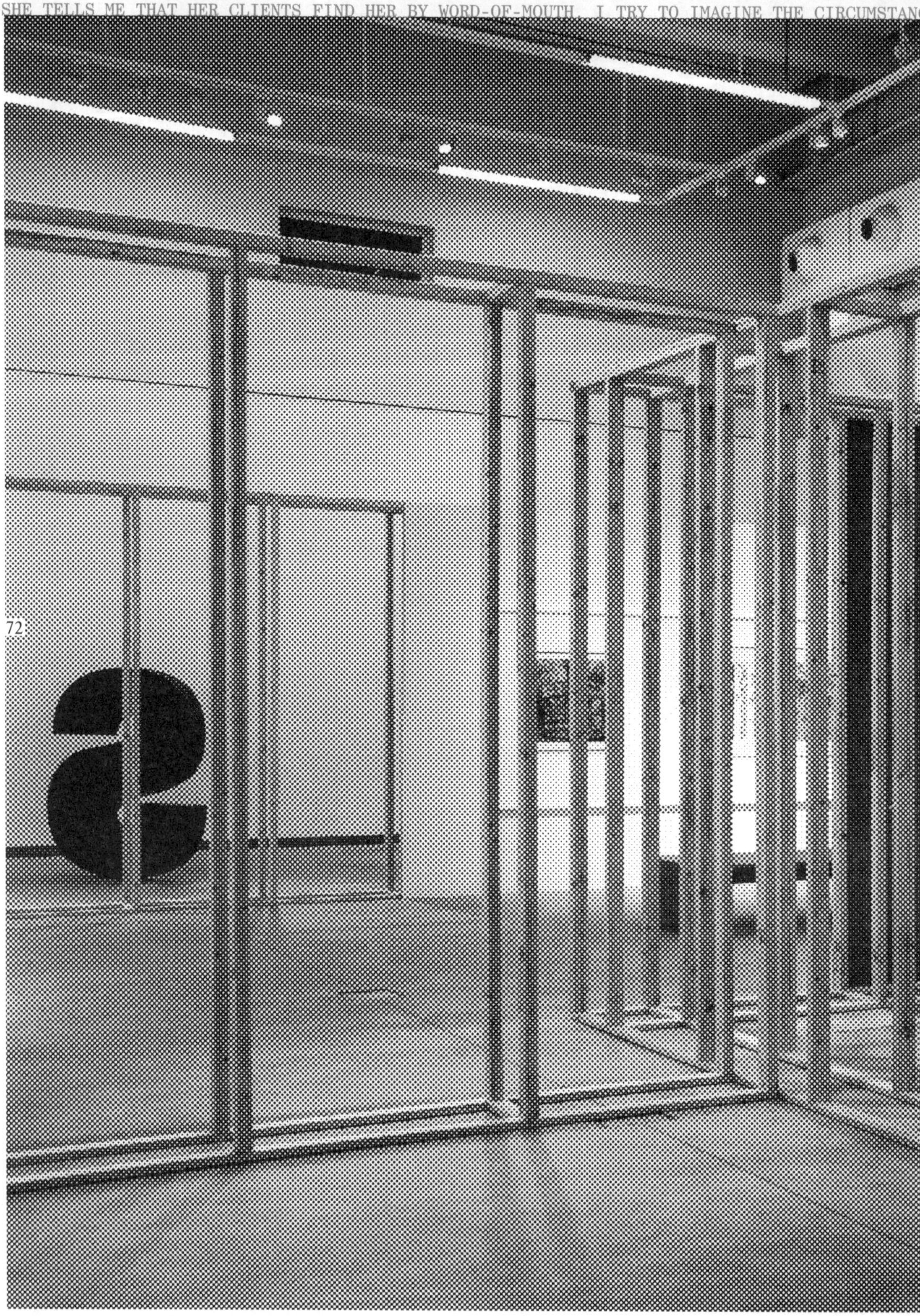

OULD LEAD TO ONE PERSON TELLING ANOTHER PERSON ABOUT SOMEONE WHO THEY CAN HIRE TO HOLD THEM. M

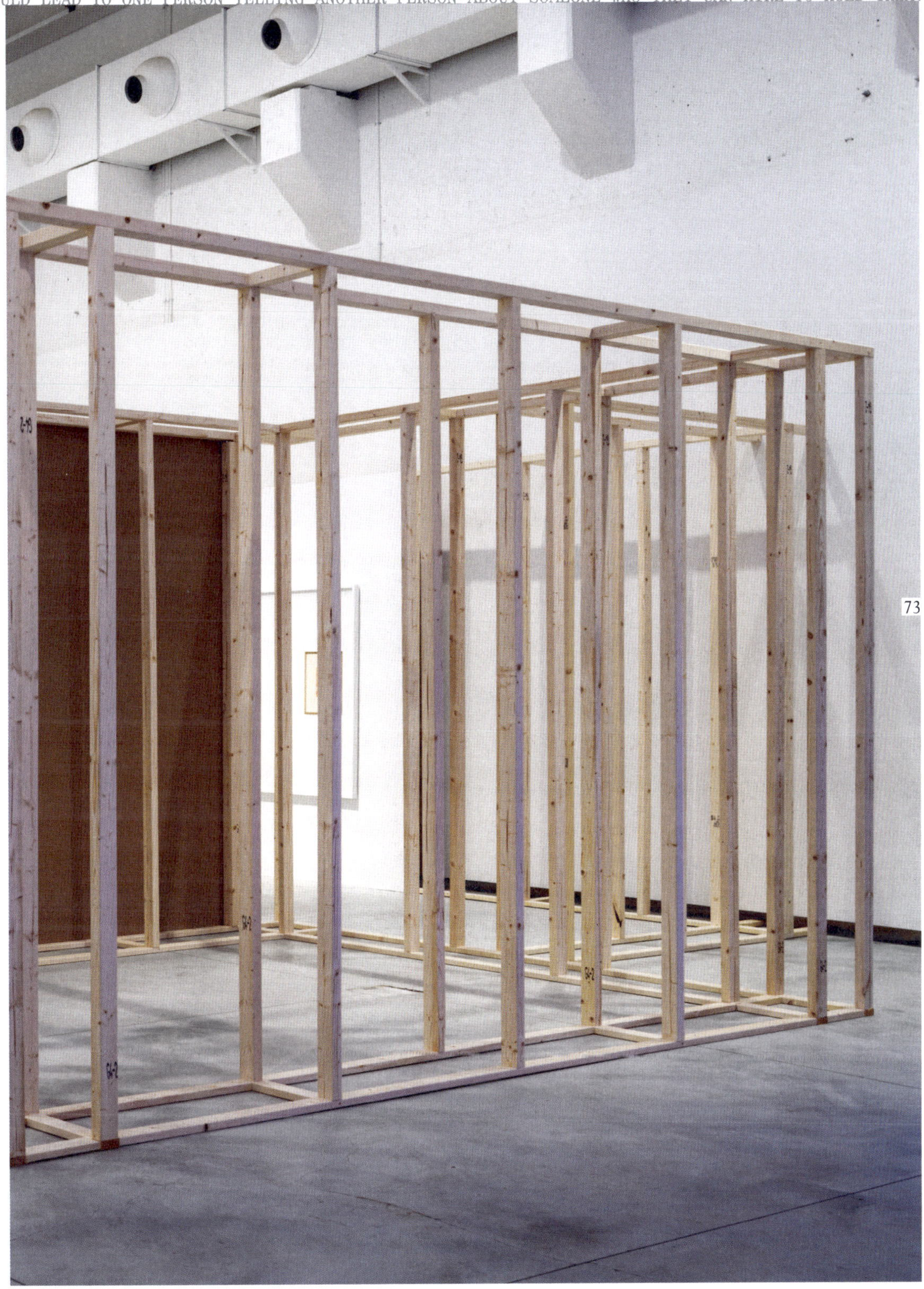

T NEIGHBOR EXPLAINS HOW MANY OF HER CLIENTS ARE YOUNG MEN WHO WORK IN THE TECH INDUSTRY. ALL

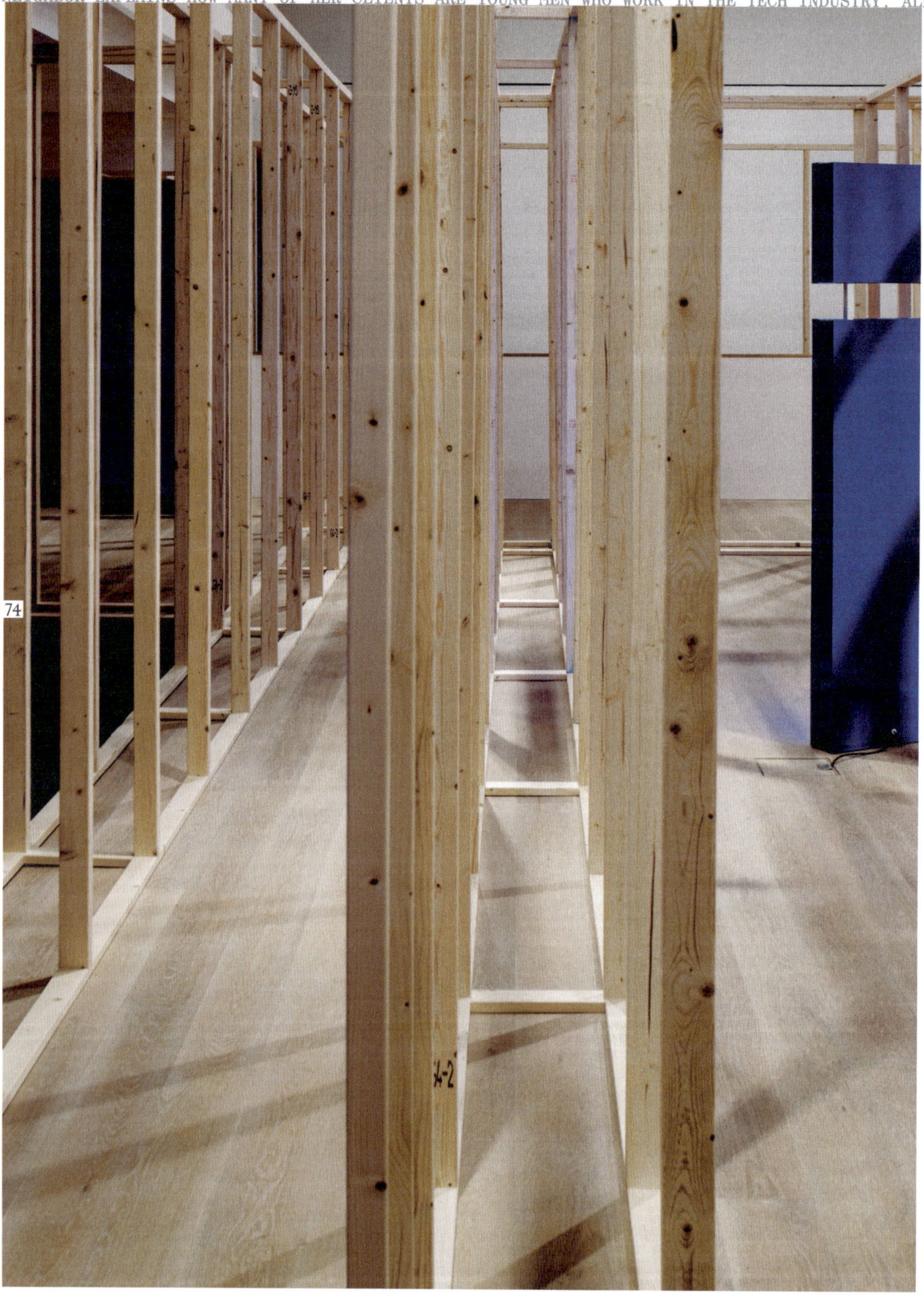

IS WORK. THEY HAVE MONEY. PORN TAKES CARE OF SEX. THEY MIGHT HAVE FAMILIES IN FAR AWAY PLACE

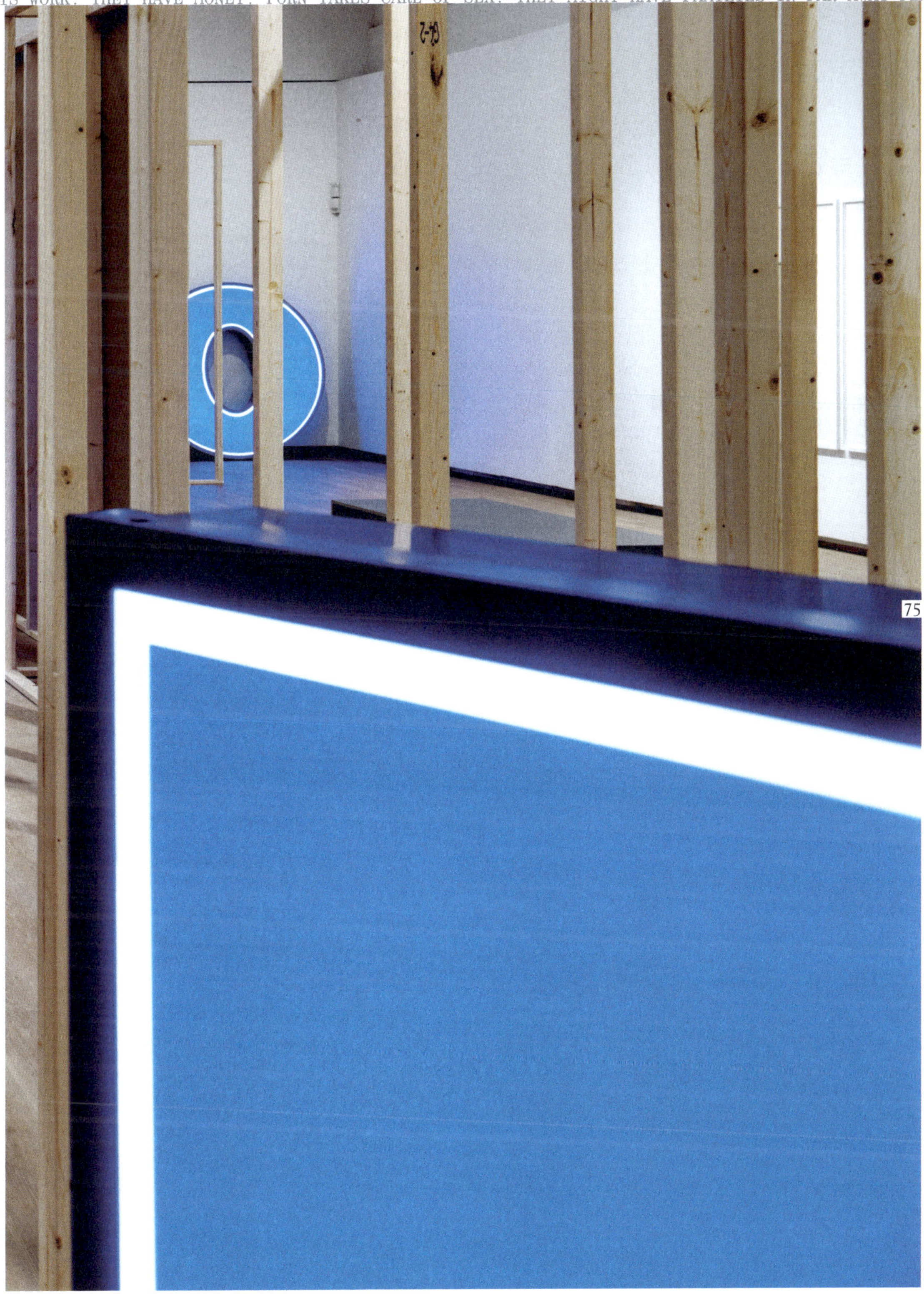

EY LONG TO BE TOUCHED IN A WAY THAT MAKES THEM FEEL CARED FOR BY ANOTHER HUMAN BEING. I FEEL

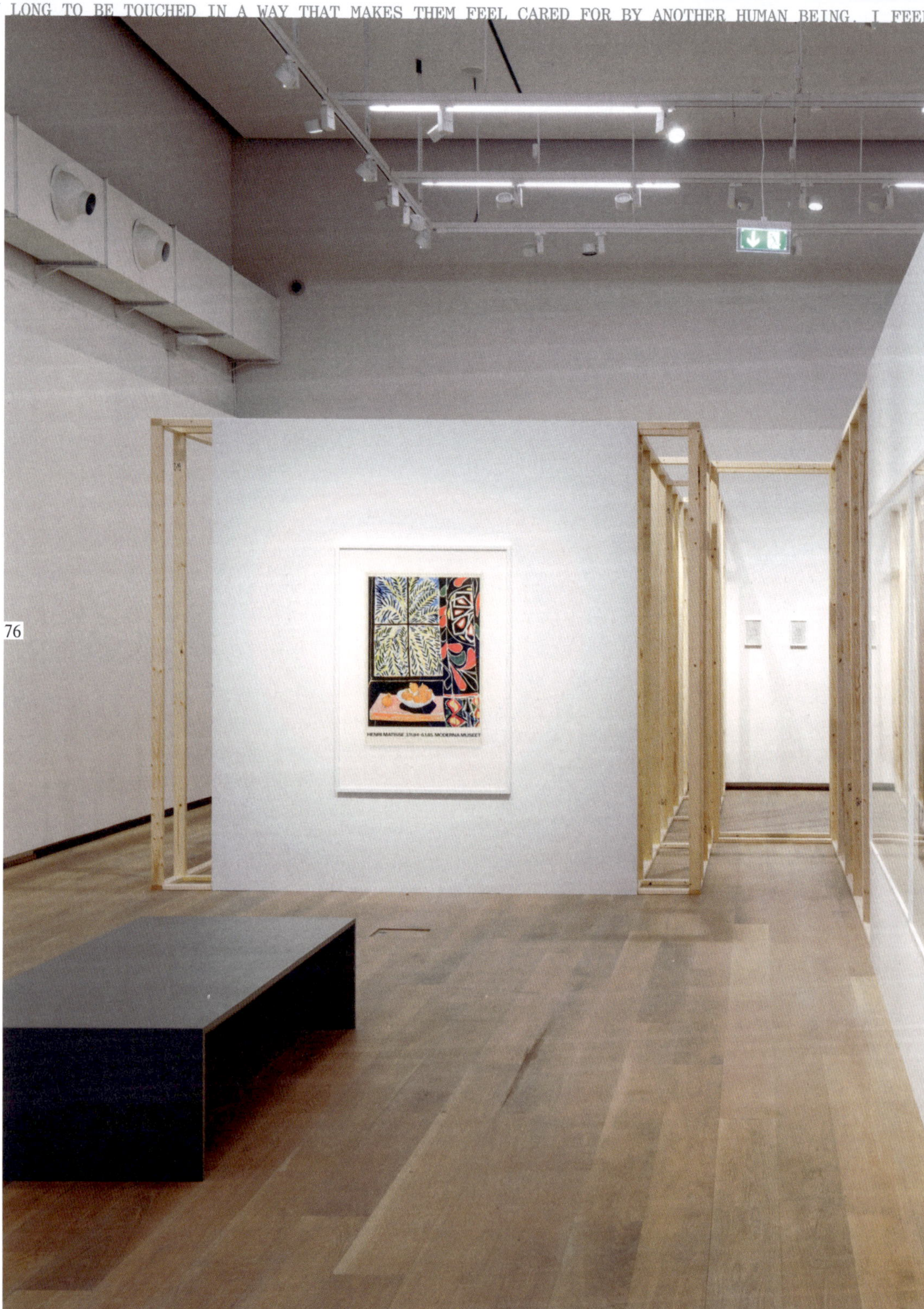

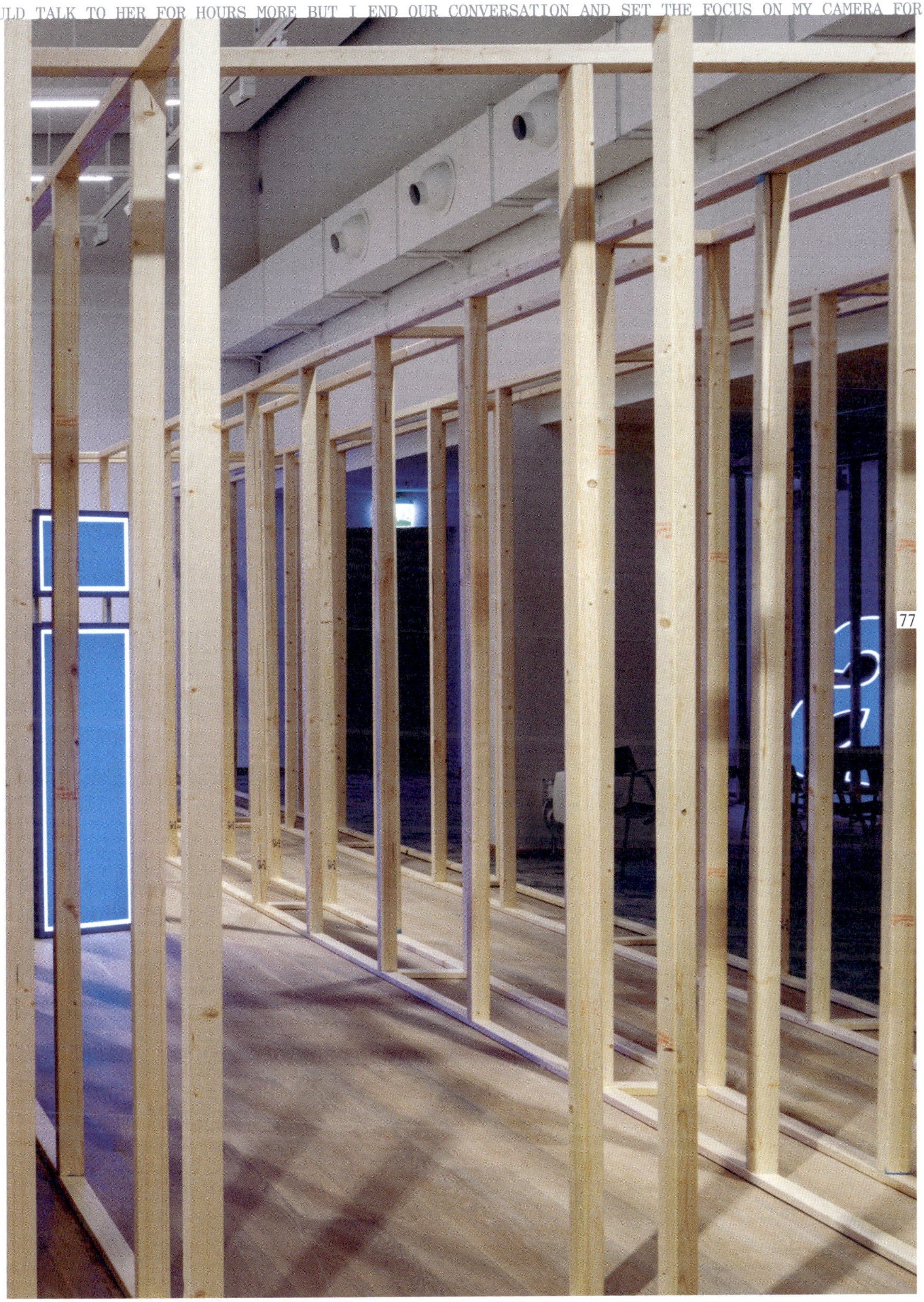

ENE BELOW, EVEN THOUGH AT THIS POINT I ALREADY KNOW THAT FOR A SECOND TIME IT'S NOT GONNA WOR

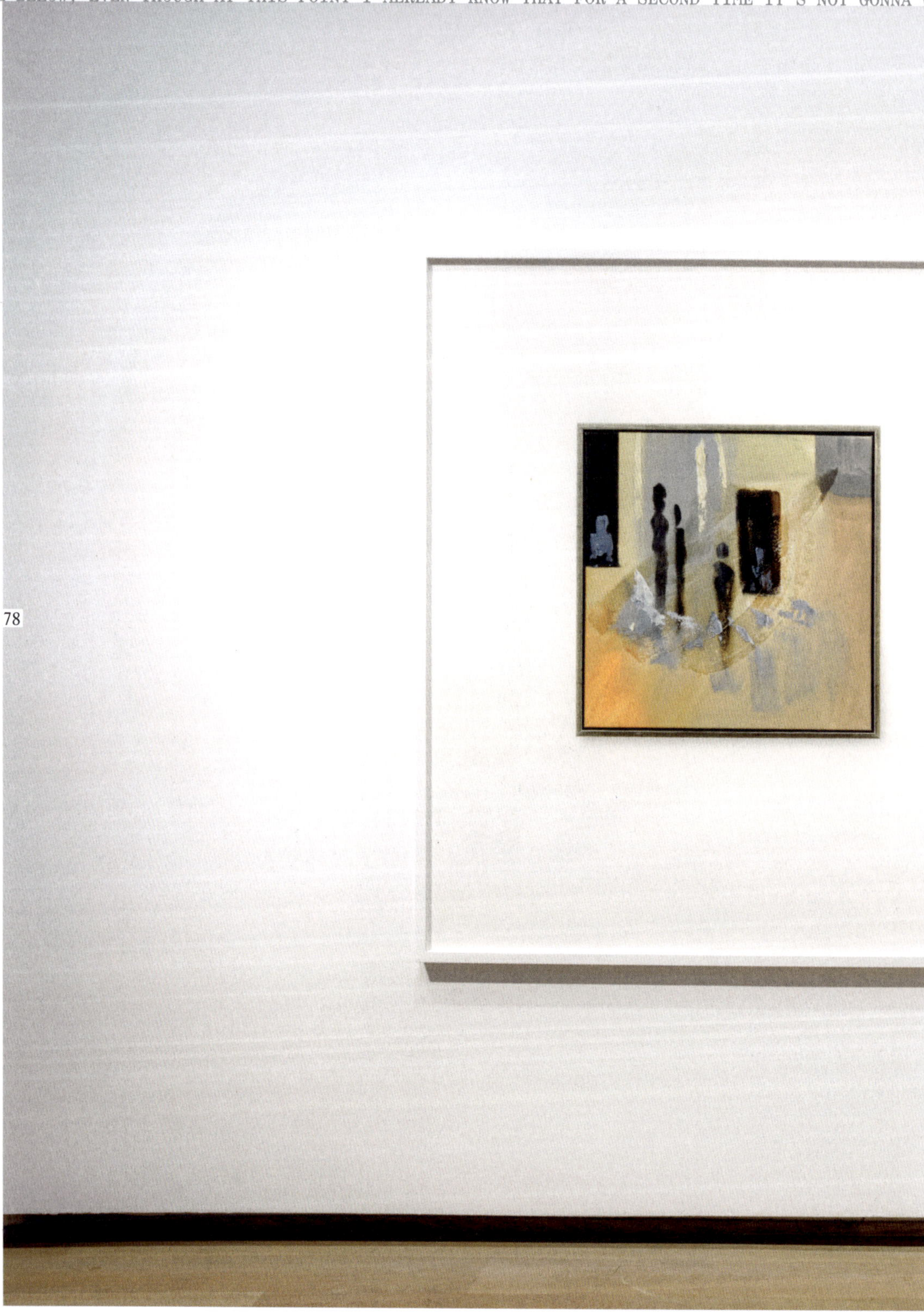

THE PLANE LANDS AT 8 PM, WHICH IS FORTY-FIVE MINUTES EARLIER THAN SCHEDULED. IT'S STILL WAY

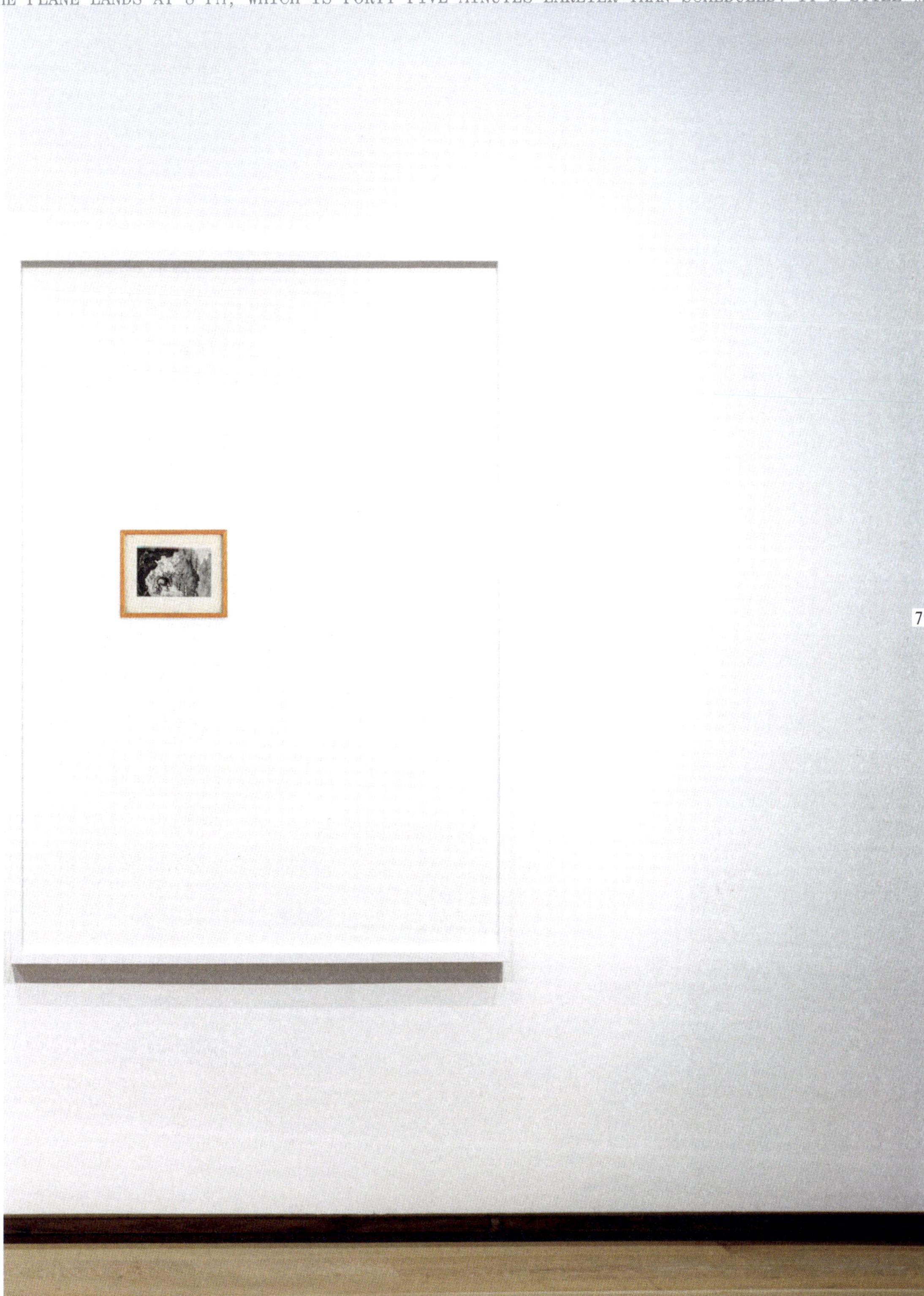

IGHT. I SEE AN EXPLOSION HERE AND THERE BUT IT'S NOTHING I CAN USE. BUT THAT'S WHEN I START

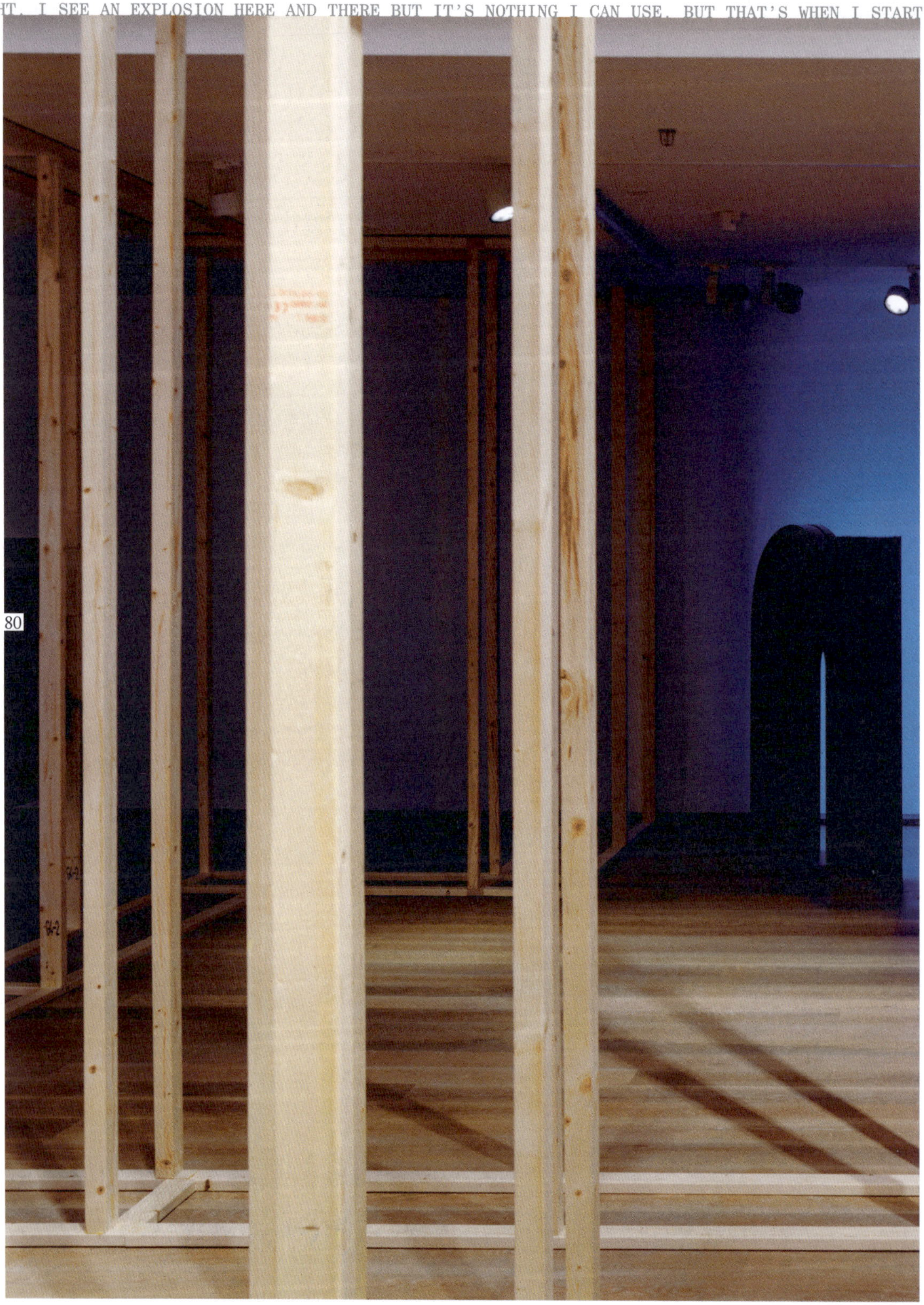

CT WHAT I'M DOING TO ANOTHER KIND OF VIOLENCE, ONE THAT IS SOFTER INVISIBLE AND PERHAPS SELF

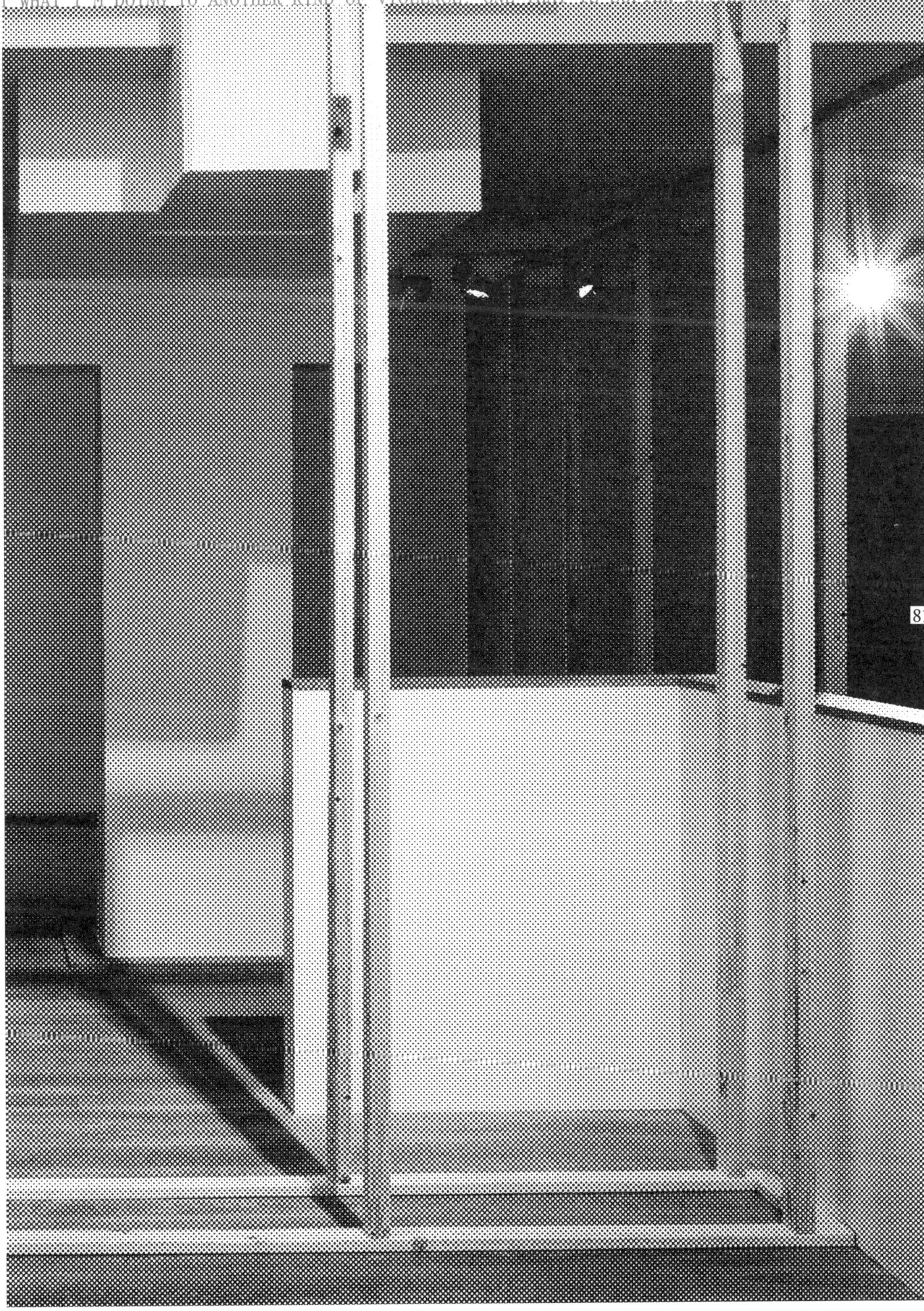

WN. FOR OTHERS, IT BECOMES ONE LONG WAKING NIGHTMARE. THE FEAR AND ANXIETY IS RAW DURING T

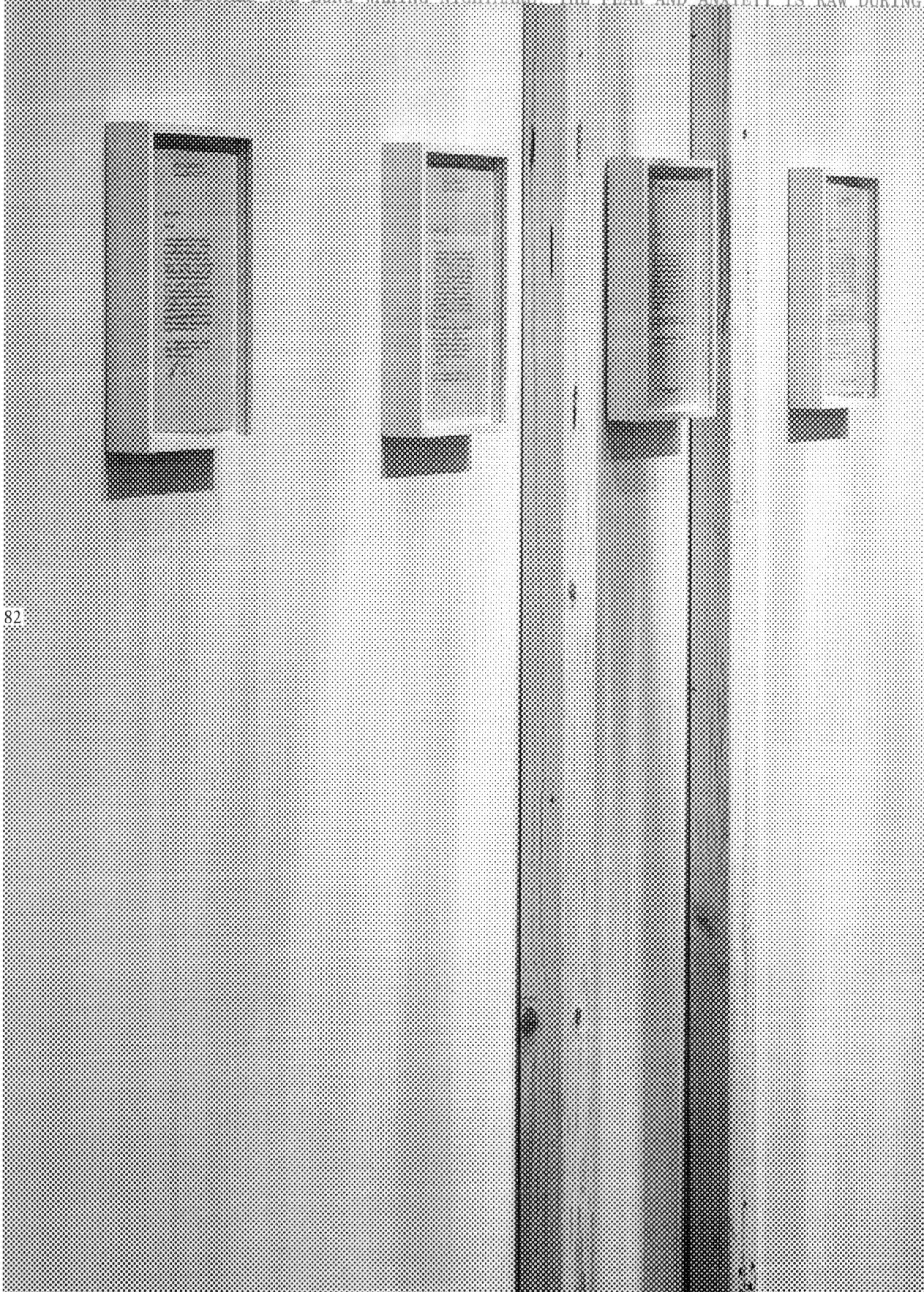

82

WAVE. BUT I NEED TO TRAVEL FROM STOCKHOLM TO EL PASO WHERE MY MOTHER IS. SHE'S SOLD THE HOUS

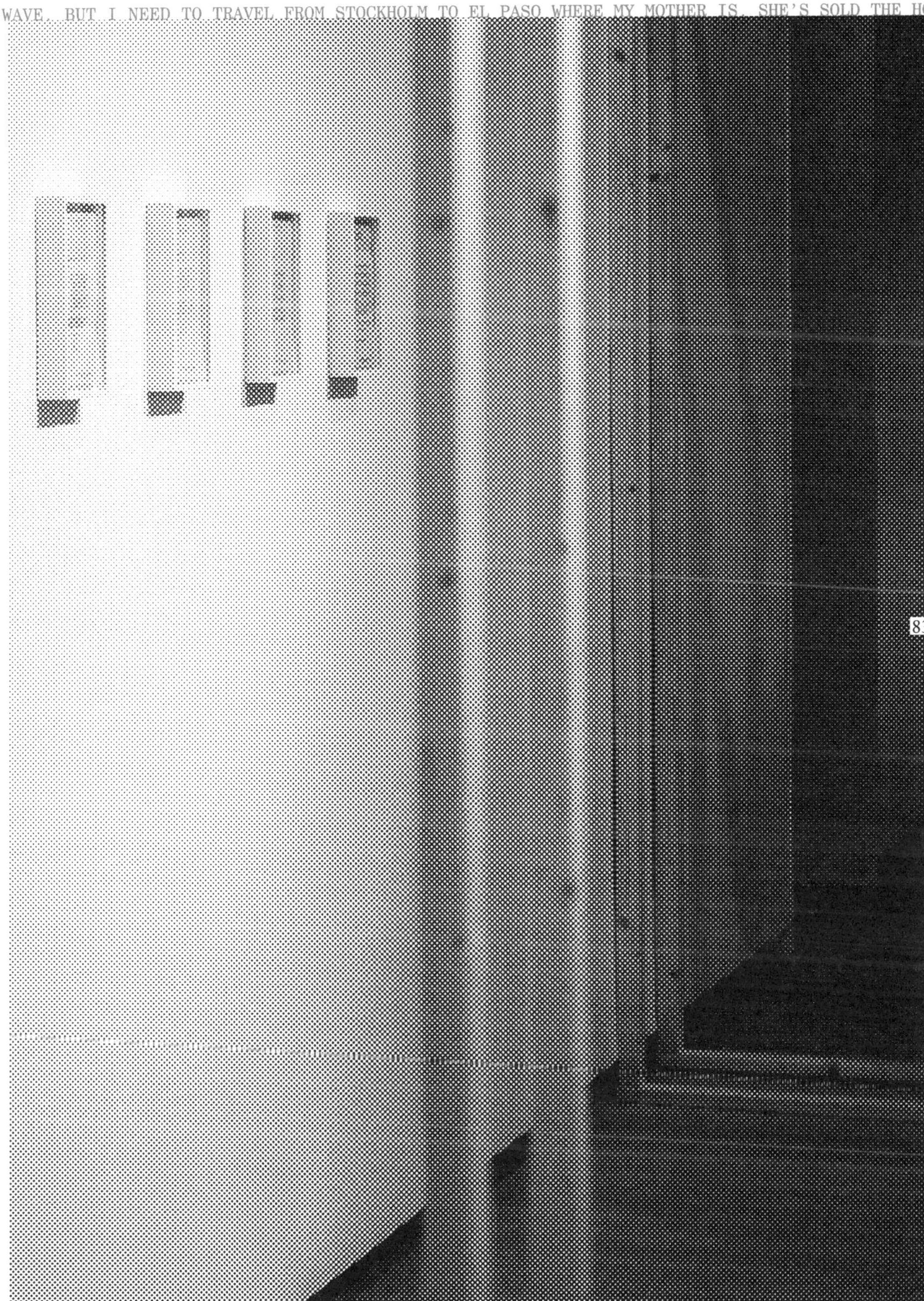

LICTED. [SOUND FROM INSIDE AN AIRPLANE] JULY FOURTH, TWENTY-TWENTY. BY THE SUMMER OF THIS YEAR

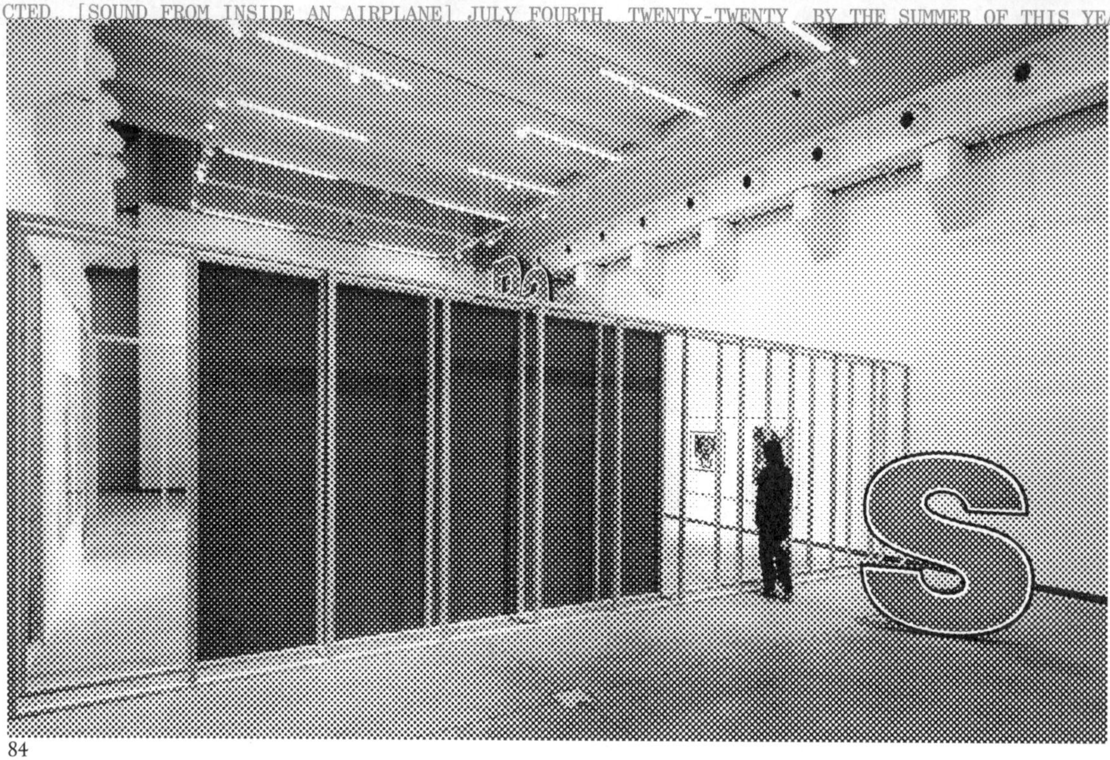

S HAVE DRASTICALLY CHANGED. FOR SOME THE CORONAVIRUS TURNS OUT TO BE A BREAK. A CHANCE TO S

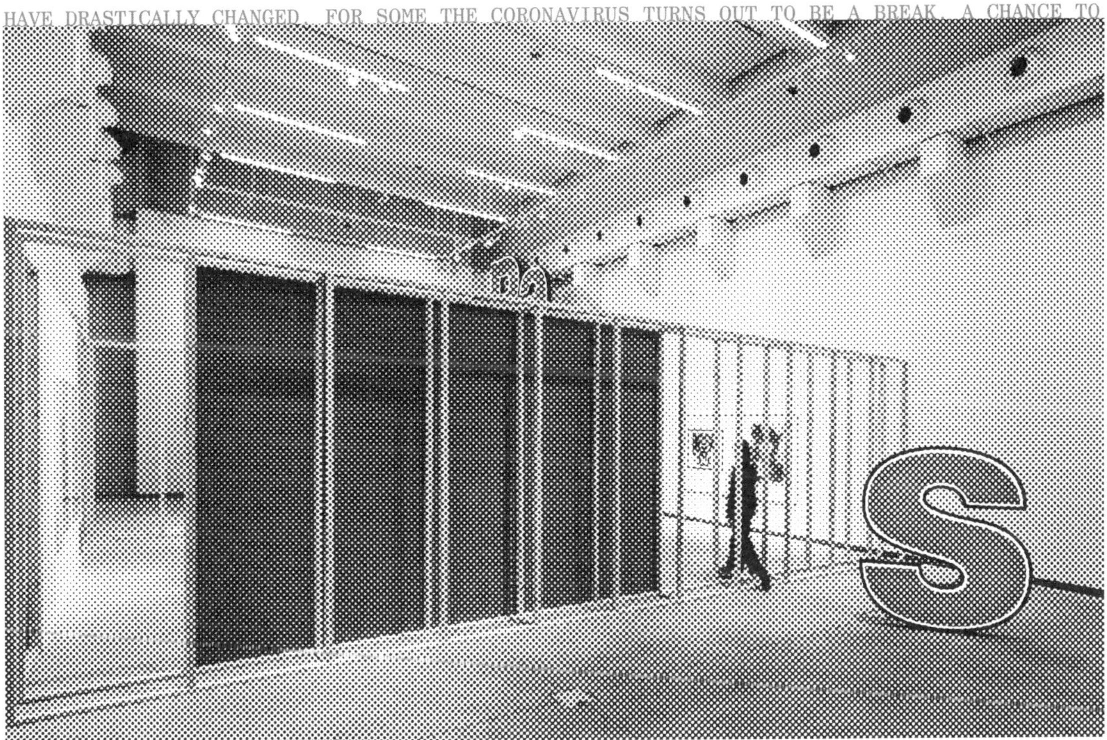

OND. STORES ARE BOARDED UP. IT'S AN ELECTION YEAR OF EXTRAORDINARY CONSEQUENCE. THREE MILLION

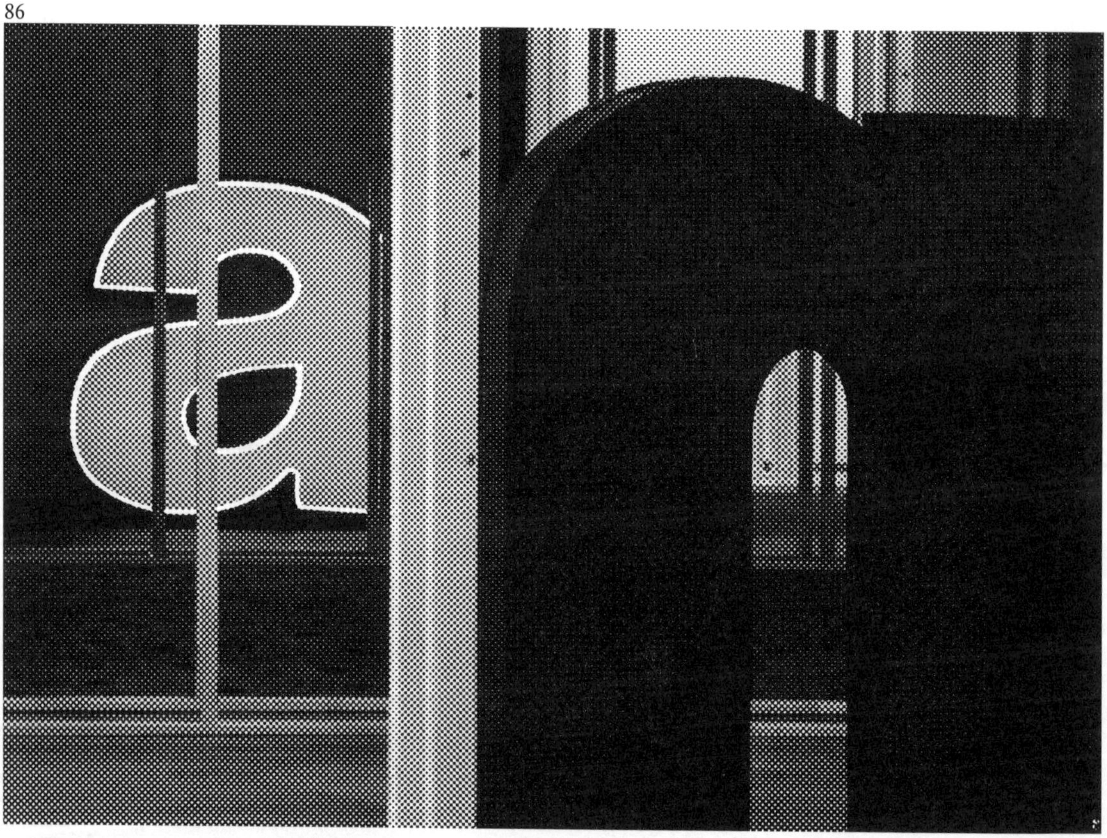

S THAN USUAL HAVE BEEN SOLD. I ARRIVE, SELF-QUARANTINE, MOVE MY MOTHER AND GET HER SITUATED B

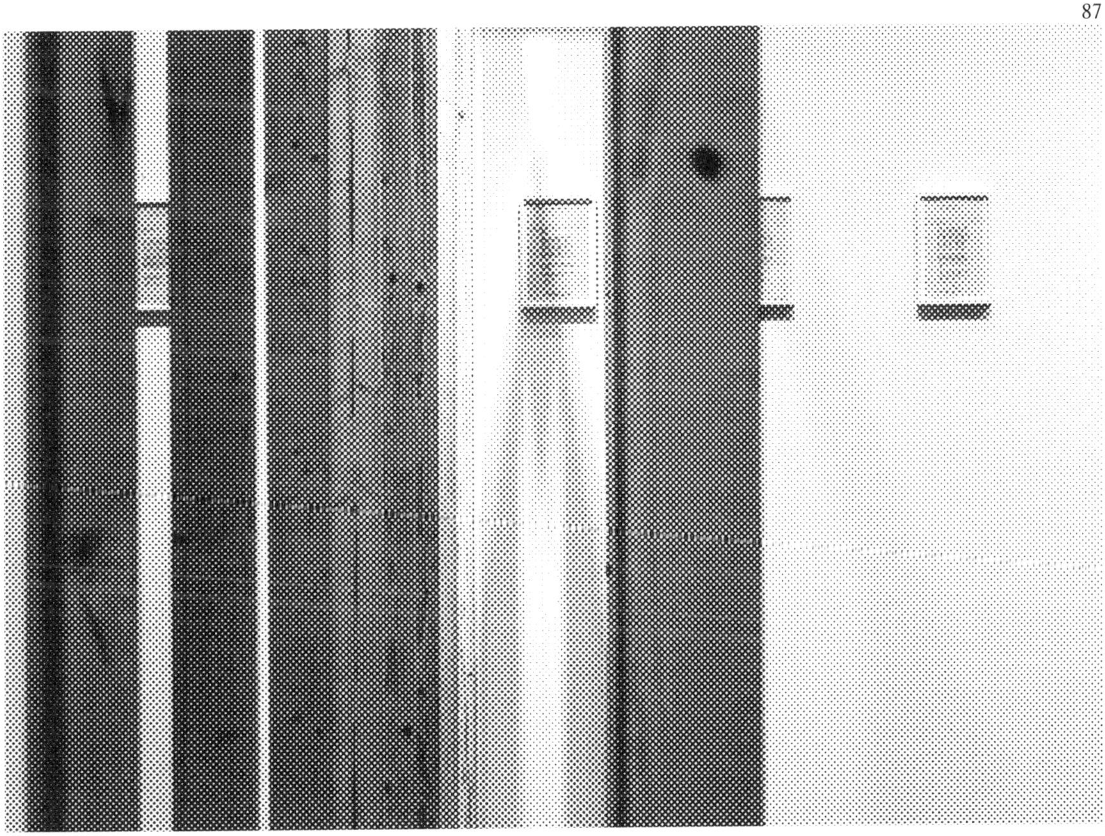

AT SHE'S LIVED IN FOR FORTY YEARS AND NEEDS MY HELP TO MOVE TO ANOTHER CITY. BY THE TIME I ARR

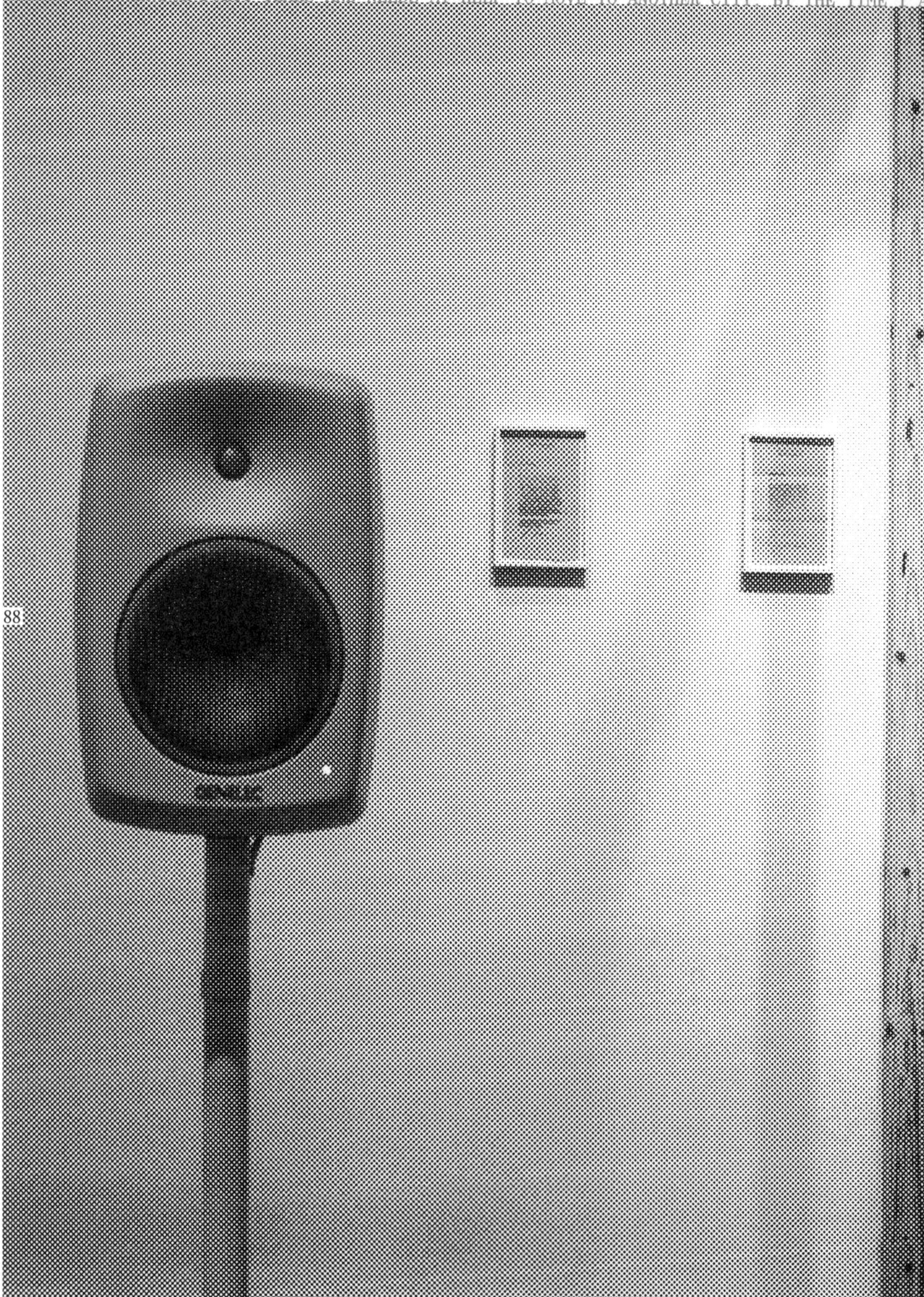

000 PEOPLE IN THE US HAVE DIED FROM THE VIRUS. BLACK LIVES MATTER PROTESTS SPAN THE COUNTRY A

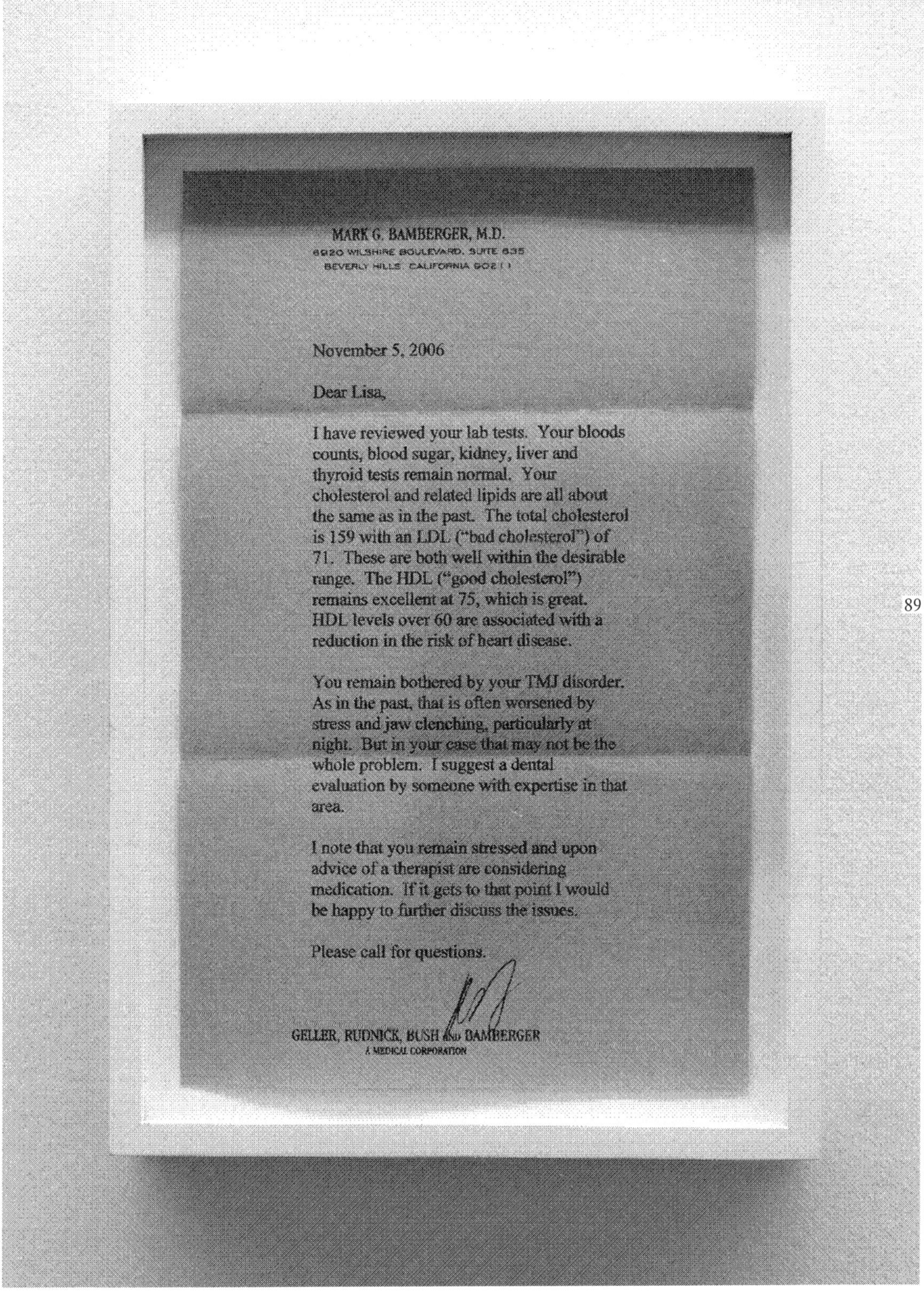

MARK G. BAMBERGER, M.D.
8920 WILSHIRE BOULEVARD, SUITE 635
BEVERLY HILLS, CALIFORNIA 90211

November 5, 2006

Dear Lisa,

I have reviewed your lab tests. Your bloods counts, blood sugar, kidney, liver and thyroid tests remain normal. Your cholesterol and related lipids are all about the same as in the past. The total cholesterol is 159 with an LDL ("bad cholesterol") of 71. These are both well within the desirable range. The HDL ("good cholesterol") remains excellent at 75, which is great. HDL levels over 60 are associated with a reduction in the risk of heart disease.

You remain bothered by your TMJ disorder. As in the past, that is often worsened by stress and jaw clenching, particularly at night. But in your case that may not be the whole problem. I suggest a dental evaluation by someone with expertise in that area.

I note that you remain stressed and upon advice of a therapist are considering medication. If it gets to that point I would be happy to further discuss the issues.

Please call for questions.

GELLER, RUDNICK, BUSH AND BAMBERGER
A MEDICAL CORPORATION

OTS. WHEN THEY ARRIVE, I SMILE WIDELY BEHIND MY MASK HOPING THEY CAN SEE IT IN MY EYES AND I A

ACCELERATOR AT STOCKHOLM UNIVERSITY

Richard Julin
artistic director at Accelerator

Accelerator is an exhibition space where contemporary art, science, and social issues meet. Its mission is to engage actively with society, producing exhibitions of international and Swedish contemporary art. Central to the institution are the dialogues we have with artists, their work, and the exhibitions we develop together. Accelerator is run by Stockholm University and is driven by an ambition to contribute toward a transparent and empathetic society by opening up opportunities for art to spark discussions and interdisciplinary dialogue.

Accelerator also runs the Art + Research program, dedicated to collaborations between our artistic team and Stockholm University researchers whose work relates to the issues and themes explored in our exhibition program. These collaborations result in public programs comprising lectures, discussions, and seminars in which artists, researchers, students, and the general public are invited to participate.

Lisa Tan's exhibition *Dodge and/or Burn*, with its daring and rigorous proposal, has been embraced by a large, engaged public audience, including researchers at the university, artists, and arts professionals. Her invitation to let visitors create their own paths through a system of open walls reflects Accelerator's aim to be a place where one is encouraged to experiment.

ABOUT THE ARTIST

LISA TAN
traces the contours of life as it is shaped by desire and determined by the contingent encounters that form it. To do this, she draws from an array of disparate associations: properties of certain natural phenomena, biographical details of one or two literary figures, violent encounters that recall others, and many more mobilizing triggers. Her process is initiated by an intuitive sense for how a situation or question that is personal in nature, when imbued with feeling, develops into a conversation on subjectivity and its relation to language, its impact on society, and its resonance in a world of others. Her work takes the form of installation, photography, video, and writing, among other gestures. Marked by material and conceptual precision, it considers the frame and conditions in which it appears and meets an audience in a manner that often engenders the work itself with its physical features and content.

Lisa Tan lives in Stockholm, Sweden. She is Professor of Art at Konstfack University of Arts, Crafts and Design. Born in Syracuse, Upstate New York, Tan was raised in El Paso, Texas, where her family settled. Tan received an MFA from the University of Southern California, Los Angeles, where she lived for several years before moving to New York. In 2012, she relocated to Sweden to undertake a practice-based PhD at HDK-Valand at the University of Gothenburg. Tan's work has been presented in solo and group exhibitions at institutions such as Kunstinstituut Melly (Rotterdam), Moderna Museet (Stockholm), Tabakalera (San Sebastián), MIT List Visual Arts Center (Cambridge), Kunsthall Trondheim, ICA Philadelphia, Kadist (Paris), and Artists Space (New York). She was included in *The Ghost Ship and the Sea Change*, the 11th Göteborg International Biennial for Contemporary Art (2021), *Why Not Ask Again?*, the 11th Shanghai Biennale (2016), and *Surround Audience*, the New Museum Triennial (2015). *Dodge and/or Burn* at Accelerator is Tan's first solo exhibition at an institution in Sweden.

OF THEM'S OPENLY CRYING, SO I MOVE TO GIVE THEM SPACE. I STAND NEXT TO THE GATE AND WAIT FOR

CONTRIBUTORS

ASIER MENDIZABAL

is an artist and Professor of sculpture at KKH, Royal Institute of Art, Stockholm. The representations of the collective, the construction of identities and the role of technique in these phenomena recur throughout his work. His practice confronts conventional narratives of history assigned to archival or ethnographic objects, as well as subcultural representations, observing their political, technical and material conditions. Writing is a common instrument in his work, always in relation to sculpture as a practice and a genealogy. Mendizabal has exhibited individually in Museo Reina Sofía, MACBA and Raven Row, and collectively in Vienna Secession, Guggenheim Bilbao, Museu Serralves, Manifesta 5 and the Venice, São Paulo and Taipei biennials, among others.

CHARLOTTA BJÖRKLIND

is a practicing child, youth and adult psychoanalyst, member of the Swedish Psychoanalytical Association (IPA). She is a teacher and supervisor at the Psychoanalytical Association's Institute and at the Department of Psychology at Stockholm University. Also a member of the editorial board of *Divan – journal for psychoanalysis and culture*, the Swedish Psychoanalytical Association's publication series, and former editor-in-chief of the EPF Bulletin (European Psychoanalytic Federation). As a writer, she has participated in the anthology *Vad är en kvinna: språk, materialitet, situation* [What is a woman: language, materiality, situation] (Daidalos, 2021) and *Freud och dödsdriften* [Freud and the Death Drive] (Tankekraft, 2021), as well as contributed to numerous Swedish and international journals.

HAYTHAM EL-WARDANY

is a writer and translator. He lives and works in Berlin. His latest book, *Jackals and The Missing Letters* (Al-Karma, 2023), considers forgotten expressions of hope within Arabic fables, where animals speak and humans listen, in a moment of post "Arab Spring" speechlessness. In previous publications, including *The Book of Sleep* and *How to Disappear*, el-Wardany has examined the potential of passivity, through regimes of listening and the dialectics of sleep and vigilance. Forthcoming is *Things That Can't Be Fixed*, a short story collection. He is the recipient of the Keith Haring Fellowship in Art and Activism 2022/2023 at Bard College.

ING MY WAY TO LOS ANGELES. I CAN'T ASK ADRIAN TO RISK INFECTION FROM THE FLIGHT OR ANYBODY EL

LIST OF WORKS

94

PROMISE OR THREAT, 2023
Site-specific construction in wood and carpet
Based on Fig. 9 in *Migraine* (2012) by Oliver Sacks, first published in 1970 by the University of California Press, Berkley and Los Angeles, California as *Migraine: The Evolution of a Common Disorder.*

DODGE AND BURN, 2023
Two-channel HD video with three-channel sound
20 minutes on a 30 minute loop (installation version)

PA, 2023
Custom-made signage in acrylic and LED light
9 individual characters in total

LETTERS FROM DR. BAMBERGER, 2001–2012
Printed ink on paper in artist's frames
Physician's reports following general medical examination
9 letters in total

WAITING ROOM SERIES, 2019
12 pigment prints on acid free cotton paper in artist's frames:

WAITING ROOM OF A PSYCHOLOGIST
(Paul Klee, With Two Dromedaries and One Donkey, 1914/19)
WAITING ROOM OF A PSYCHOLOGIST
(Leonardo da Vinci, Study for the face of Saint Anne, 1500)
WAITING ROOM OF A PSYCHOLOGIST
(Paul Klee, Himmelsblüten über dem gelben Haus, 1917)
WAITING ROOM OF A PSYCHOLOGIST
(Henri Matisse, Cup of Oranges, 1916)
WAITING ROOM OF A PSYCHOLOGIST
(John Wipp, Blåe, date n/a)
WAITING ROOM OF A NEUROLOGIST
(Claude Monet, The Water Lily Pond: Green Harmony, 1899)
WAITING ROOM OF A NEUROLOGIST
(Terence Warren, Welcome Intrusion and A Snip in Time, 1979)

WAITING ROOM SERIES, 2023
12 pigment prints on acid free cotton paper in artist's frames:

WAITING ROOM OF A PSYCHOANALYST
(Henri Matisse 3.11.84–6.1.85 Moderna Museet)
WAITING ROOM OF A PSYCHOANALYST
(Christian Boltanski 5 Sep–14 Dec 2008 Magasin 3 Stockholm Konsthall)
WAITING ROOM OF A PSYCHOANALYST
(Raden del, v.d.K. sculps., La Roche Percee Big Tête Noire, blz. 184)
WAITING ROOM OF A PSYCHOANALYST
(n/a shadow figures and door)
WAITING ROOM OF A PSYCHOANALYST
(Louvieres, tapisserie conçue, réalisée en flandres a halluin, France)

FIREWORKS. THE CAPTAIN TELLS ME HE'LL TRY BUT THAT ONCE WE GET INTO LA AIR SPACE, HE'LL HAVE

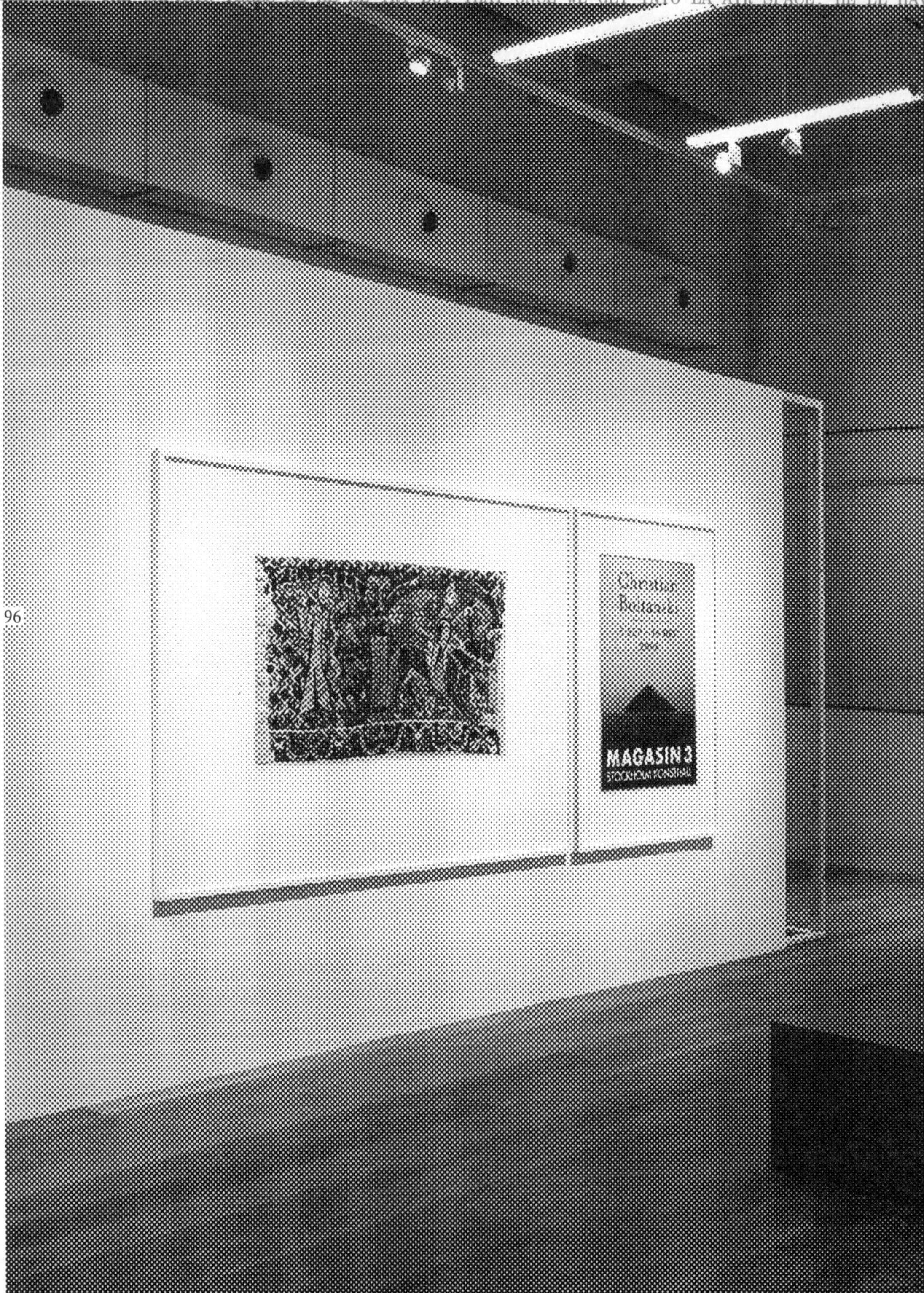

HATEVER AIR TRAFFIC CONTROL TELLS HIM. IN THE AIR, I CAN SENSE THAT WE'RE GOING MORE SLOWLY. I

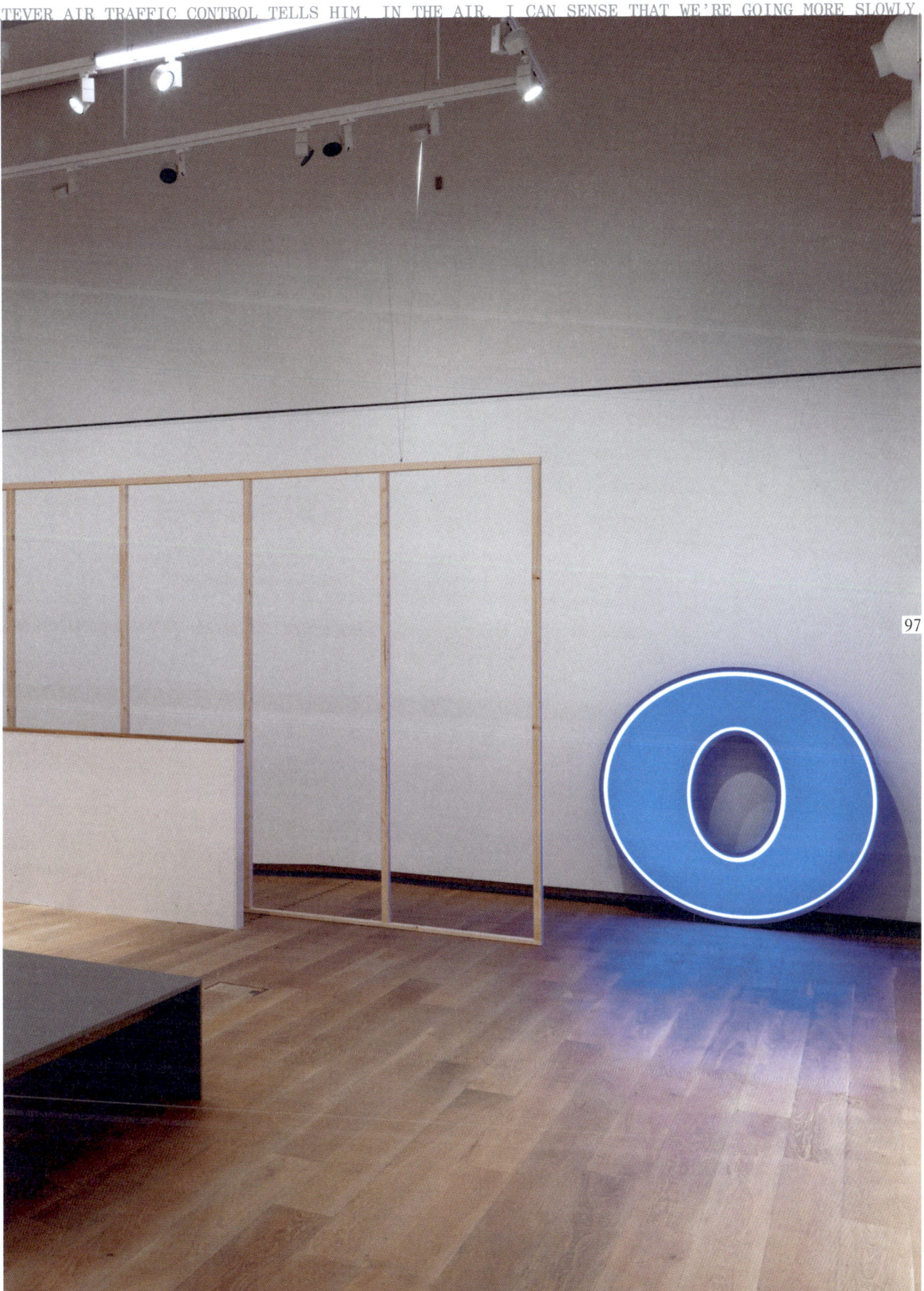

TING DARK. MY CAMERA IS READY. THE NEWS HAS BEEN REPORTING MUCH HIGHER THAN USUAL SALES OF ILI

98

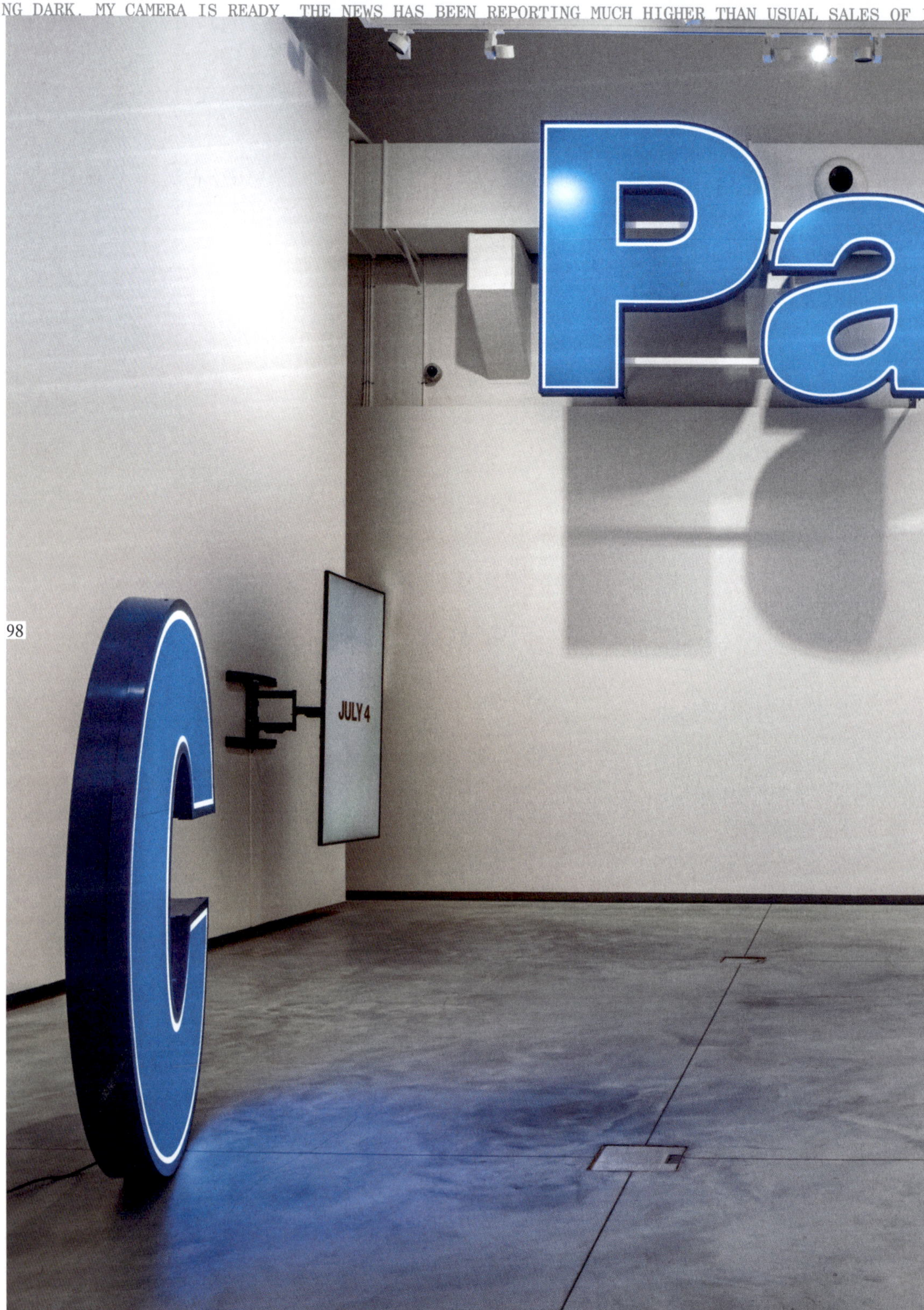

REWORKS. FIREWORKS HAVE BEEN EXPLODING IN LA LATE AT NIGHT SINCE JUNE. UNINTERRUPTED SLEEP IS

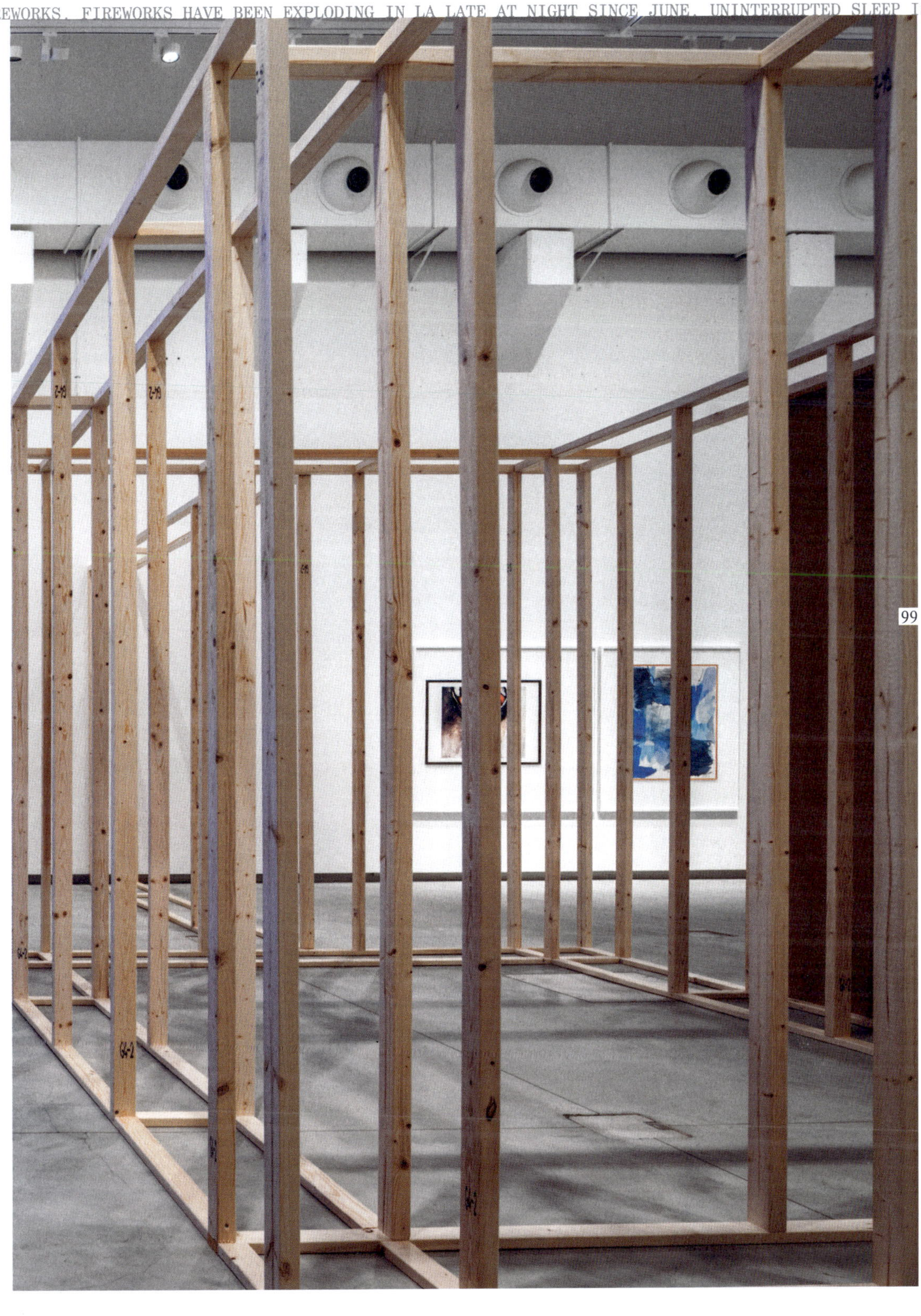

E BY. THEORIES CIRCULATE THAT IT'S A RIGHT-WING STRATEGY TO UNNERVE BLACK LIVES MATTER PROTEST

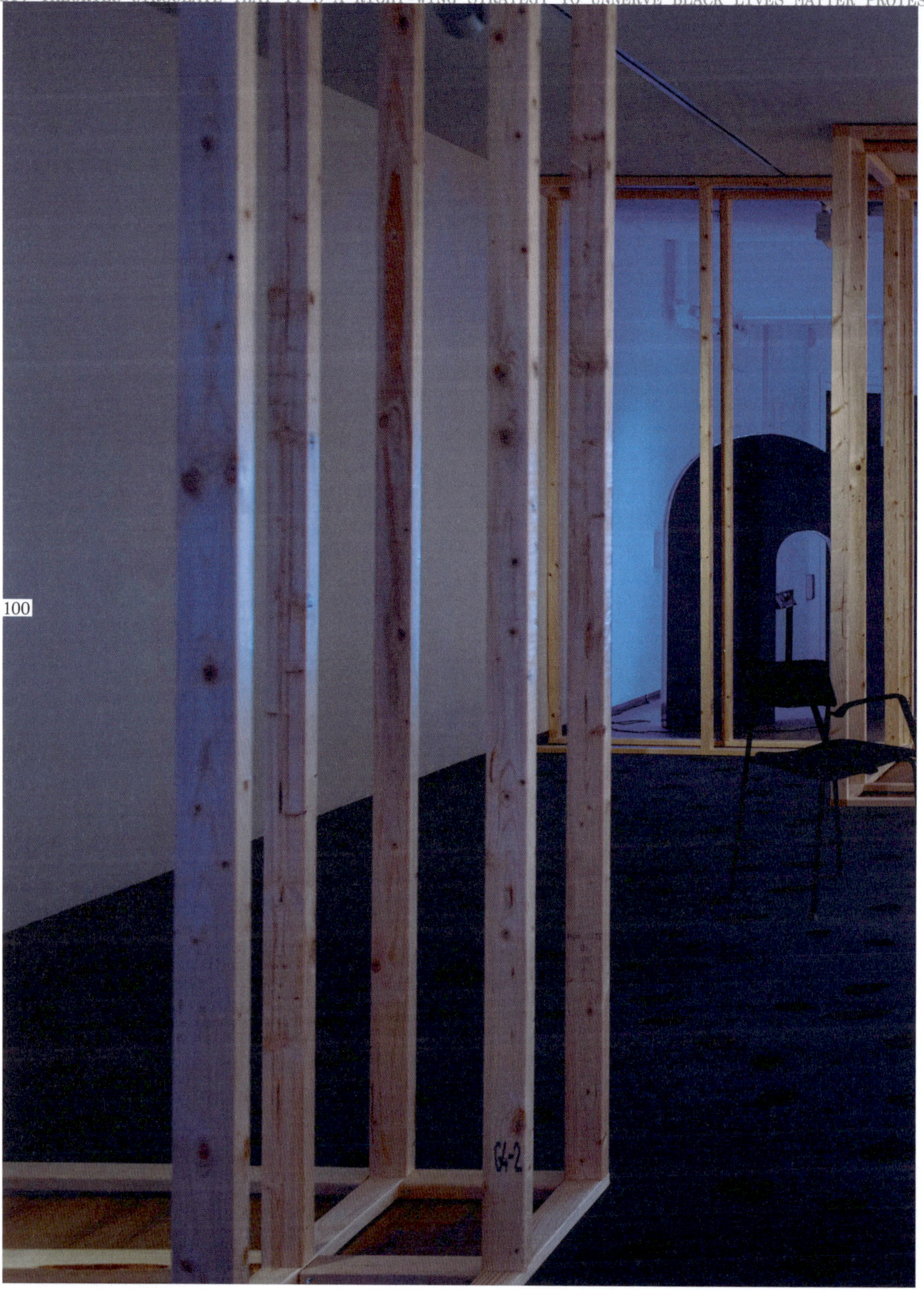

100

WE GET CLOSER THE PLANE CONTINUES TO FLY NEXT TO THE OCEAN. WE'RE SUPPOSED TO TURN LEFT TO LI

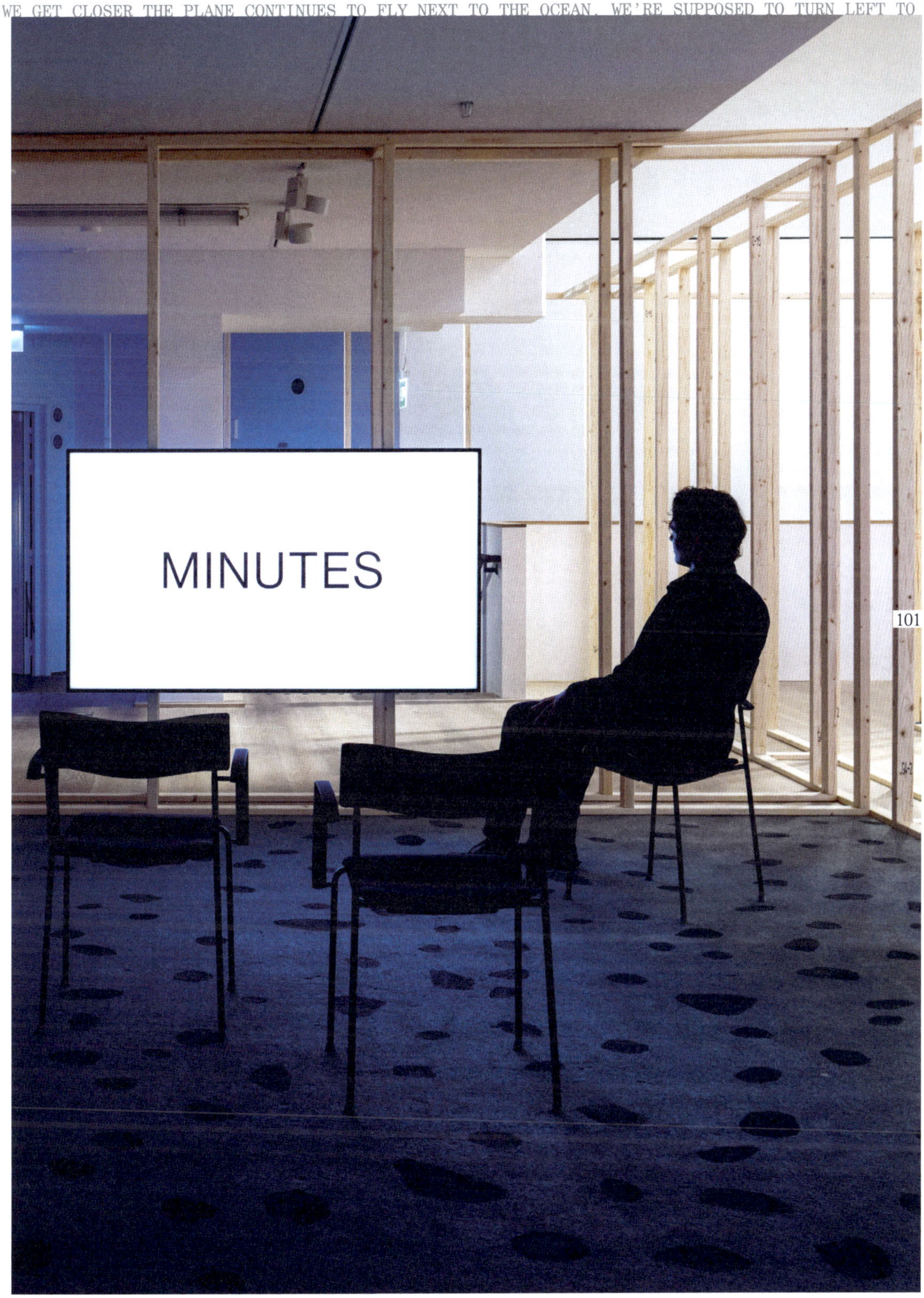

This book is published on the occasion of the exhibition:
Lisa Tan *Dodge and/or Burn*

Accelerator, Stockholm, Sweden
September 16, 2023 – February 11, 2024

CURATED BY Therese Kellner

ARTISTIC DIRECTOR Richard Julin
ADMINISTRATIVE DIRECTOR Mårten Snickare
CURATOR Therese Kellner
EXHIBITION TECHNICIAN Birt Berglund
COMMUNICATIONS MANAGER Erica Moon-Nam Lindberg

Accelerator is part of Stockholm University. The exhibition program is supported by Magasin III Museum for Contemporary Art and the Robert Weil Family Foundation.

PUBLISHED AND DISTRIBUTED BY
Mousse Publishing
Contrappunto s.r.l.
Via Pier Candido Decembrio 28,
20137, Milan–Italy

AVAILABLE THROUGH
Mousse Publishing, Milan
moussemagazine.it
DAP | Distributed Art Publishers, New York
artbook.com
Les presses du réel, Dijon
lespressesdureel.com
Antenne Books, London
antennebooks.com
Idea Books, Amsterdam
ideabooks.nl
LibroCo, Florence
libroco.it

PUBLISHING EDITOR Ilaria Bombelli
GRAPHIC DESIGN Anna Azzali
TEXTS BY Therese Kellner, Charlotta Björklind, Asier Mendizabal, Haytham el-Wardany, Richard Julin, Lisa Tan
TRANSLATIONS BY
FROM SPANISH TO ENGLISH Beatriz Llenín Figueroa (Asier Mendizabal)
FROM SWEDISH TO ENGLISH Karen Diamond and Hans Ohlsson (Therese Kellner and Charlotta Björklind)
FROM ARABIC TO ENGLISH Katharine Halls (Haytham el-Wardany)

Appearing throughout the book is a transcript of the voice-over from Lisa Tan's *Dodge and Burn* (2021–2023)
COPYEDITING Sriwhana Spong

PHOTO CREDITS (IF NOT INDICATED OTHERWISE)
Jean-Baptiste Béranger, © 2024 Accelerator, Stockholm University
ILLUSTRATION PAGE 7 Oliver Sacks, *Physiological Organisation of Migraines*. Reprinted from Sacks, *Migraine* (London: Picador, 2012), 203. Reproduced by permission from The Oliver Sacks Foundation
PHOTOGRAPH PAGE 89 © 2019 Adrian Bugge

FIRST EDITION 2024

PRINTED IN ITALY BY Industrie Grafiche Pacini, Pisa

ISBN 978-88-6749-614-3

€ 25 / $ 30

This catalogue was produced with the support of Stiftelsen Längmanska kulturfonden and Gunvor och Josef Anérs stiftelse.

Lisa Tan would like to thank Asier Mendizabal, Beatriz Llenín Figueroa, Charlotta Björklind, Ellie Ga, Haytham el-Wardany, Johanna Gustafsson-Fürst, Jonas Dahlberg, Katharine Halls, Sarah Demeuse, and most of all Therese Kellner.

ACCELERATOR
Stockholm University

AL ROUTE. BEFORE LEAVING THE AIRCRAFT THE PILOT FINDS ME TO TELL ME THAT OURS IS THE FIRST FLIGHT OF THE NIGHT AND PERHAPS THE FIRST EVER TO BE DIVERTED BECAUSE OF THE FIREWORKS. THEY'RE SO INTENSE THAT IT'S DANGEROUS. I DRIVE AWAY FROM THE AIRPORT INTO TOTAL CHAOS. HEADING UP THE 110 FREEWAY THAT BISECTS SOUTH LOS ANGELES. THE EXPLOSIONS DISSIPATE AFTER DOWNTOWN AND AS I CONTINUE IN THE DIRECTION OF HOLLYWOOD INTO NEIGHBORHOODS WITH HIGHER INCOME BRACKETS. THE NEXT DAY AN ACRID YELLOW HAZE BLANKETS THE ENTIRE CITY. AUTHORITIES SAY THAT THE POLLUTION FROM THE FIREWORKS IS HAZARDOUS. PEOPLE ARE ADVISED TO STAY INSIDE WITH THE WINDOWS CLOSED. [VOICE OF FLIGHT ATTENDANT OVER INTERCOM] – *WE DIDN'T FLY OVER THE CITY* WE CAME IN OVER THE WATER SO YOU CAN'T REALLY SEE 'EM WELCOME TO LOS ANGELES *PLEASE REMAIN SEATED WITH YOUR SEATBELTS FASTENED AND ALL YOUR CARRY-ON ITEMS RIGHT WHERE THEY ARE UNTIL WE ARRIVE AT THE GATE AND THE CAPTAIN TURNS OFF THE FASTEN SEAT BELT SIGN BE CAREFUL OPENING UP THE OVERHEAD BINS . . . IT'S BEEN A PLEASURE SERVING ALL OF YOU TODAY DRIVE SAFELY, COME FLY WITH US AGAIN SOON IT'S A FAIRLY LONG TAXI, WAIT HERE JUST BE PATIENT AS SOON AS THE CAPTAIN TURNS OFF THAT FASTEN SEAT BELT SIGN YOU CAN GET UP AND GET YOUR BELONGINGS ONCE AGAIN, THANK YOU* [END CREDITS] DODGE AND BURN VIDEO LISA TAN EDITING LISA TAN AND NILS FRIDÉN SOUND ENGINEERING PHILIPP CONRAD MAP GRAPHICS GOOGLE EARTH